National Alliance for
Grieving Children

When Someone Dies
A Child-Caregiver Activity Workbook

by the National Alliance for Grieving Children

Copyright © 2016 by National Alliance for Grieving Children

All rights reserved. This book or any portion thereof may not be reproduced or used in any manner whatsoever without the express written permission of the publisher except for the use of brief quotations in a book review or scholarly journal.

First Printing: 2016

9 8 7 6 5 4 3 2

ISBN: 978-0-9963804-0-9

National Alliance for Grieving Children, 3500 N A ST STE A-2, Midland, TX 79705

www.ChildrenGrieve.org

Ordering Information:

Special discounts are available on quantity purchases by corporations, associations, educators, and others. For details, contact the publisher at the above listed address.

U.S. trade bookstores and wholesalers: Please contact National Alliance for Grieving Children Tel: (866) 432-1542

Table of Contents

A Message of Hope to Parents/Caregivers, 6
A Message of Hope to Kids, 7
My Someone Who Died, 8
Memories Last Forever, 9
A Lasting Impression, 10
Alike and Different, 11
Remembering Your Person, 12
Draw Anything, 14

UNDERSTANDING DEATH AND REMEMBERING WITH RITUAL

Death is a Part of Life, 16
What Do You Think? 17
When People Die, 18
What's That? 19
The Funeral/Memorial Service, 20

WHAT IS GRIEF LIKE?

Grief is Like, 22
My Grief is Like, 23
My Grief: Agree or Disagree, 24
Feelings are Physical, 26
Feelings Factory, 27
Grief is Full of Surprises, 28
Rainy Days Happen, 30
The Twists & Turns of Grief, 32

MY SUPPORT...HOW I COPE WITH GRIEF

My Family, 34
I Am Supported, 35
I Am Brave, 36
All Kinds of Changes, 38
I Never, I Wonder, I Wish, 39
It's Okay to Feel Sad, 40

It's Ok to Feel Mad, 42
Calming Exercise, 43
Fear, 44
Bringing Fears to Light, 46
Big Energy Activities, 47
I Like & Dislike, 48

GRIEF AT SCHOOL AND WITH FRIENDS

Grief At School, 50
What School is Like for Me, 51
Hurtful Words, 52
Responding to Hurtful Words, 53
Helpful Words, 54
What Comforts You? 55
Draw Anything, 56

SPECIAL DAYS AND REMEMBERING MY PERSON

Special Days & Holidays, 58
Remembering...My Way, 60
Remembering...As a Family, 61
A Letter to Your Person, 62
A Letter from Your Person to You, 64
Map of Grief, 66
Draw Anything, 68
A Year in Review, 69
Game Time! 70

Closing Message to Kids, 72
Closing Message to Parents/Caregivers, 73
Common Questions From Parents/Caregivers, 73
About the National Alliance for Grieving Children, 76
Credits & Acknowledgements, 77
Contributions, 78

A Message to Parents/Caregivers Raising Bereaved Children

If you are in possession of this book, it is likely that you and your child are grieving the death of someone important to you. This activity book was created with bereaved children and their parent/caregiver in mind. Our hope is that the information and suggested activities contained within these pages will provide insight that will help you better understand how grief impacts children, and how to create the best home environment to promote health and healing for you and your child. The suggestions we offer and the activities we designed are for the purpose of providing you and your child the opportunity for positive interaction.

The good news is that with the right kind of support, children are fully capable of successfully navigating the challenges of bereavement and growing into healthy adults. As a matter of fact, research has found that healthy children are the product of a positive relationship with their parent or caregiver, especially where there is care and warmth, modeling of healthy coping behaviors, honest and open communication, and clearly established expectations for behavior in the home.

This activity book strives to provide you with opportunities to interact with your child in positive ways, while acknowledging your grief and how you are both coping with the changes brought about by the death of someone in your life.

In the margins and throughout these pages we have strategically placed suggestions to provide you with good information about childhood grief and how to help children. If you have multiple children in your home, please remember that each one of them is experiencing grief in their own unique way. So, allowing similarities and differences in their expressions as you participate in these activities is perfectly acceptable. A variety of reactions from your child is to be expected, including sadness, anger, even laughter and joy. The most important thing to remember is that you are one of the most valuable resources your child has in their life, and you have a great opportunity to help them grow even in the midst of their (and your) grief.

© National Alliance for Grieving Children 2016

A Message to Kids:

It can be hard when someone dies. It can be difficult to share thoughts and feelings. This book has been given to you and your parent/caregiver to help your family remember, talk about, and honor your person. Nothing can bring the people in our lives who have died back, but remembering them, talking about your memories, and sharing your feelings can be helpful to you and your family. You can work on these activities on your own, or with the help of your parent or caregiver. Either way we hope you find the activities in this book helpful, supportive, and encouraging.

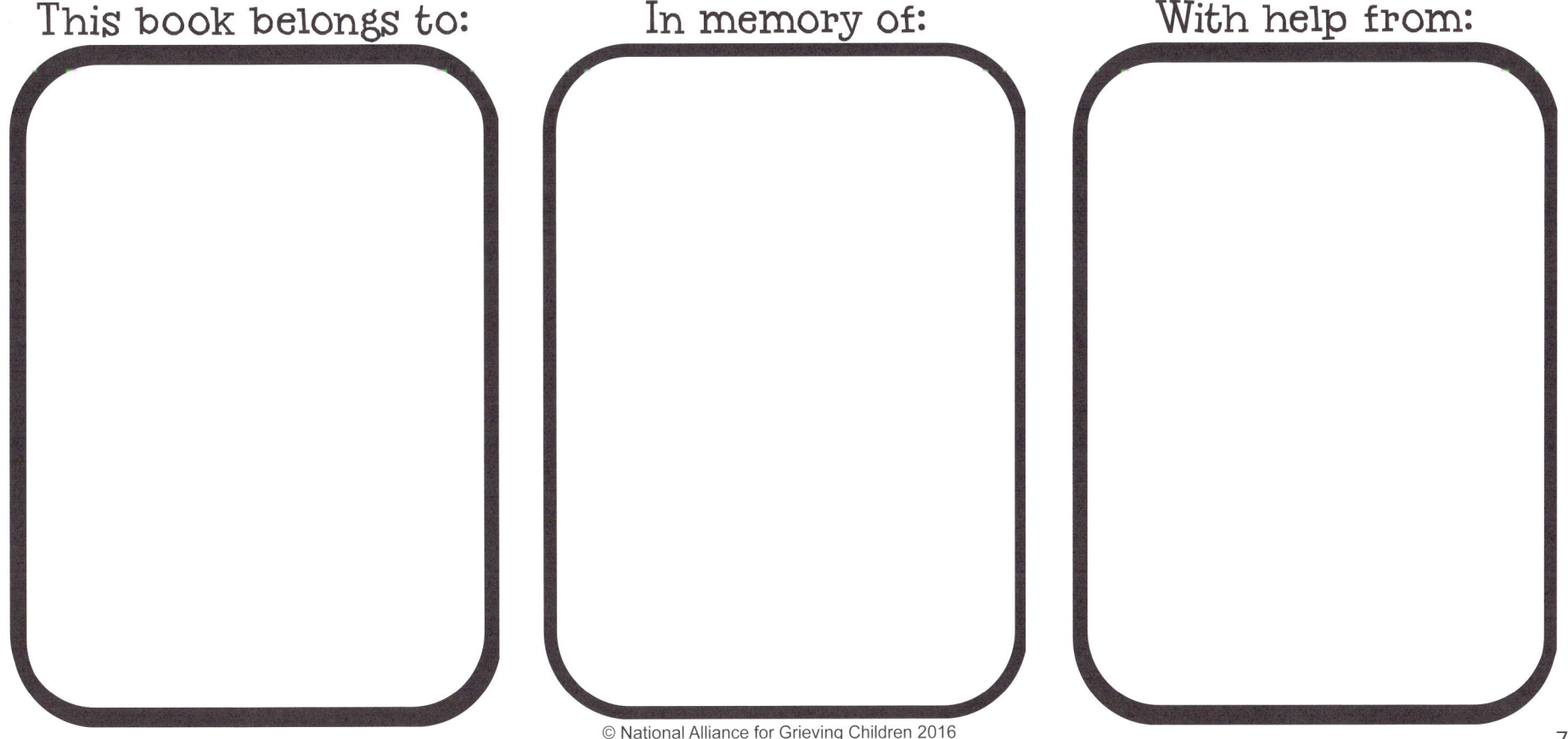

This book belongs to:

In memory of:

With help from:

© National Alliance for Grieving Children 2016

Parent Tip:
Talking about the deceased can be helpful. A death ends a life but the relationship remains. This page provides an opportunity for you and your child to begin to talk about the person who died. This would be a perfect time to share your favorite stories about something your person did that you remember the most.

Children love to hear stories about the people in their lives- funny stories, meaningful stories, even stories about how their person faced challenges in life.

My Someone Who Died

ACTIVITY TIME: Attach a photo or draw a picture of your person who died.

© National Alliance for Grieving Children 2016

Memories Last Forever

Just because someone dies, it does not mean we forget them.

ACTIVITY TIME: Write your person's name on the sash and color the picture as you like in honor of them.

Parent Tip:
Do you need help knowing how to talk to your grieving child? A good rule of thumb is to keep it simple and to follow their lead.

Additional tips are included at the back of this book. Take a few moments to flip to the frequently asked questions pages and review the information shared by professionals.

This activity gives children the opportunity to create a memorial for the person who died. Creating a memorial provides a context for children to begin to express their thoughts and feelings about the person who died.

At first, remembering the person who died can be difficult for children, but as they have the occasion to remember and reflect in a safe setting with loving adults in their lives, remembering their person becomes easier and cherished.

© National Alliance for Grieving Children 2016

Parent Tip:
This is a good time to think about and talk about the lasting impressions the person being remembered has made in your life.

Some children may need time to think about this concept of a "lasting impression" before being able to share their own thoughts.

You can help your child understand what a lasting impression is by sharing examples with them about how your person left impressions on your life.

If they cannot think of a way their person has left a lasting impression, that's alright, move on to the next activity. Children will express their grief when they are ready to do so.

A Lasting Impression

ACTIVITY TIME: Go on a leaf hunt and find a leaf (or several). Place your leaf under this page and gently rub with a crayon across the top. You will see the pattern of the leaf appear! Try using different leaves or different crayon colors.

Extension: Add words to your picture to describe how your person impacted your life.

Always Remember: Just as the leaf has left a lasting impression on the paper, your person has made a lasting impression on you.

© National Alliance for Grieving Children 2016

Alike And Different

ACTIVITY TIME: Fill in the blanks for your and your person's favorite things. If you don't know or don't remember their favorites, ask someone else who may remember. If no one knows or remembers, choose something that reminds you of your person. Use the blank spaces to come up with your own favorites.

Parent Tip:
While it is natural for children to identify with a person who has died, children should know that they can still be themselves and that differences are not necessarily a bad thing.

This is a great opportunity to talk to your child about what makes them unique. You might share with them the things you like most about them. Celebrate their differences and let them know they are appreciated just as they are.

This could also be a great time to plan a special time together with your child doing some of their favorite things. Spending time doing things your child enjoys helps to develop a strong, trusting relationship between you and your child.

Favorite Thing:	Me:	My Person:

Parent Tip:
At first, memories about the person who died might be difficult. It is natural for children to want to avoid some of these memories, especially those that are hard to think about. As their parent/caregiver, you might be able to guess what some of these difficult memories may be, but you also might be surprised about what they remember.

Keep in mind, that children are interpreting and remembering events in their lives, often with limited understanding, and from a more concrete perspective.

You will find that there might be the need to provide clarity, which is certainly important, but, be sure to allow your child to express their memory fully before providing further insight they might need.

Remembering Your Person

Memories are a wonderful way to stay connected to your person who died, but memories can also be difficult, especially remembering changes that a person's illness might have brought. Do you have any difficult memories?

ACTIVITY TIME: List or draw some of memories that are difficult for you to think about...

© National Alliance for Grieving Children 2016

Although there may be difficult memories, there might also be favorite memories.
ACTIVITY TIME: Draw your favorite memories of your person. If you want to, cut out photos and pictures from magazines that remind you of your person and paste them here.

Parent Tip:
As your child is able to talk about and remember the person who has died, you may find that many of their memories are positive.

You can help your child to recall some of these meaningful memories by sharing some of your own memories.

Be sure to allow them to think about some special times of their own, allowing them to reflect before you share your own memories.

Use this space to draw anything you want about the person who died.

Understanding Death and Remembering with Ritual

Parent Tip:
This page provides a concrete explanation about death, including that it is universal and a natural part of life.

Young children often struggle with these concepts, so be patient with them as they come to understand better what it means that someone has died.

For example, they might not fully understand that people who die cannot come back or that they cannot go see them.

This activity also provides a wonderful opportunity for you to talk to your child about your own beliefs about life and death. Share with them from your own religious, cultural, or familial beliefs and traditions.

Death is a Part of Life

Everyone and everything that is alive will eventually die. Death is a part of life and the reaction to loss, which is called "grief", is natural.

Life and death can be seen everyday in nature. The seasons of the year reflect the life-cycle. All living things and people are born, live their lives and eventually die.

© National Alliance for Grieving Children 2016

What Do You Think?

ACTIVITY TIME: Write or draw your responses.

- Which season of the year reminds you most of birth?
- Which season of the year reminds you most of living?
- Which season of the year reminds you of most of dying?
- Which season of the year reminds you most of being dead?

Parent Tip: Since younger children are concrete thinkers, they generally have a more difficult time understanding metaphors for death.

The seasons of the year provide a wonderful example from nature about the "seasons" of our lives. You can simply take a walk with your child in nature and find many examples of how everything that lives, also dies.

To read more on how we see life and death in nature read the book Lifetimes: The Beautiful Way to Explain Death to Children by Bryan Mellonie

© National Alliance for Grieving Children 2016

Parent Tip:
This page provides a foundation for talking to your child about your own religious or family beliefs and traditions.

The information provided on this page is important because even with religious explanations, children are curious about the body, what it means for the body to die, and, very particularly, what happens to the body once it is dead.

Burial, cremation, and funerals can be confusing for children, but lose some of their mystery when time is taken to explain facts about death and the body.

When People Die

Dying is a part of living. Everything that is alive will die and that's okay.

Bodies stop working for different reasons. Sometimes bodies stop working because they get really sick, or too hurt, or too old.

When a person's heart stops beating and their body stops working, they die.

A body that is dead can no longer think, feel, or move. After a person dies, family members have a choice of what to do with the body of the person who died.

Some place the body in a casket and put the body into the earth, or mausoleum in a cemetery.

Others, have the body cremated. Cremation is a process where the body is heated to a very high temperature and is transformed into soft, powdery ashes. The ashes can be placed in an urn or scattered back into nature.

© National Alliance for Grieving Children 2016

What's That?

ACTIVITY TIME: Draw a line to match the word to its picture.

CASKET

URN

HEARSE

CEMETERY

COLUMBARIUM

MAUSOLEUM

HEADSTONE

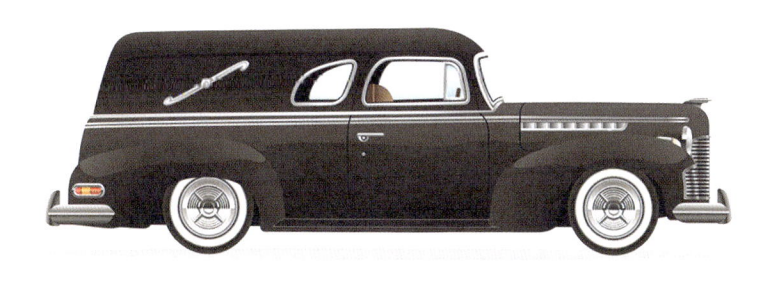

Parent Tip:
Simple, honest explanations are best to use.

For example:
Casket- *a special container that holds a body after death.*

Urn-*a special container that holds a body that has been cremated after death.*

Hearse- *a vehicle used to transport a body after death.*

Cemetery- *a place for burial of a body after death.*

Columbarium- *a place for a body that has been cremated after death.*

Mausoleum- *(or vault) an above ground place for a body after death.*

Headstone- *(or tombstone) an identifying marker in a cemetery.*

© National Alliance for Grieving Children 2016

The Funeral/Memorial Service

A question I have about the funeral/memorial service:

What I remember. Write about or draw a picture of something you remember from the day of your person's funeral or memorial service.

What is Grief Like?

Parent Tip:
Although it can be challenging to think about and talk about grief, it can also be useful to process one's feelings about what has happened.

Some children may want to talk about it and others may not. That is alright. Everyone grieves in their own way.

Processing grief does not have to be done with talking. Some children may need to first think about and gain some understanding of their own thoughts and feelings, before being able to communicate those thoughts and feelings to others.

It is important to note that children will express their grief through art, play, pretending, and other ways that feel most natural to them.

Joining your child in their play will provide a context for getting to know them better.

Grief is Like...

Have you ever jumped into a cold swimming pool? It DOES NOT feel good! In fact, many times, all you want to do is GET OUT of that cold, painful water. Imagine a cold pool that you cannot get out of.

Grief is like... a cold swimming pool that you can't get out of. You CAN sit on the side of the pool with just a toe in the water and try to imagine that the COLD water is warm and fine, but in reality it is still cold.

So if Grief is like a cold swimming pool what can you do to make it feel better?

Over time, if you can find ways to get into that pool a little at a time you will discover that by **allowing yourself to feel** the cold water, the pool water begins to feel warmer and warmer...

This is like grief. If you can find ways, over time, to allow yourself to feel the painful reality of your loss and all the feelings grief brings, those feelings can become more familiar and less shocking and disorienting.

One day you may eventually find yourself splashing around and having fun in your "grief pool". The water may still be just as cold but because you allowed yourself to feel it, you have changed.

That is why it is important to experience grief. Your world has changed and experiencing your grief (in a way that works for you) is a way to adjust to all changes that loss brings into your life.

© National Alliance for Grieving Children 2016

My Grief is Like...

ACTIVITY TIME: What does your grief looks like? Look around your house, your community, your world and think about what your grief looks like. Is it messy? Ugly? Hopeful? Whether you decide to cut pictures out of a magazine, draw, collect rocks, sticks, and leaves, or take pictures it doesn't matter. You can paint, build, or make models. Either write/draw about your grief here or take a picture of what you make and paste it here.

Parent Tip:
This exercise can be a great jumping off point towards discussing what your child is going through, what they need, and how you can be supportive.

For a younger child, you might want to help them read each one, letting them decide whether the statement applies to them or not. This is not an indicator of how "well" or "not well" your child is doing. But, it can provide helpful information to better understand what grief is presently like for them.

Understanding your child is an important part of creating a safe space for you and your child to interact and for you to offer the support, encouragement, and understanding that they most need.

My Grief: Agree or Disagree

Grief is BIG! It can affect every part of your life. Read through the following common experiences of grief and mark the ones you have been feeling.

✓ = Agree
? = Not Sure
X = Disagree

- [ ] I feel sad most of the time.
- [ ] I feel so tired since the death.
- [ ] I am easily frustrated lately.
- [ ] I have a hard time concentrating.
- [ ] I want to be alone.
- [ ] My body hurts more.
- [ ] I think it's OK to cry.
- [ ] I feel responsible for the death.
- [ ] School is hard for me since the death.
- [ ] I enjoy being around my friends.
- [ ] I want to talk more about what's happening.
- [ ] I worry about how my family members are doing.
- [ ] I feel OK, even happy, but worry that it is wrong.
- [ ] My friends don't understand what I'm going through.

© National Alliance for Grieving Children 2016

- ☐ I talk to my friends about my feelings.
- ☐ I dream about my person who died.
- ☐ I have a difficult time sleeping.
- ☐ I am good at letting my grief out.
- ☐ I would like to hang out more with my family.
- ☐ I am unsure why my person died.
- ☐ I have questions about the death.
- ☐ I forget sometimes that my person has died.
- ☐ I am angry with God.
- ☐ I'm worried someone else in my life will die.
- ☐ I am confident my person knew I loved them.
- ☐ I am mad at my person for dying.
- ☐ I think it's my fault my person died.
- ☐ I'm worried that I might die.
- ☐ Other: _____
- ☐ Other: _____
- ☐ Other: _____

Parent Tip:
Has your child shared a feeling or thought which is concerning to you? Try to not react alarmed. Gently ask what they are thinking/feeling, letting them know that any feeling they have is okay. How we feel is often out of our control. Our actions, on the other hand, are in our control and we are tasked with making healthy decisions in the midst of difficult emotions.

Explore what this looks like with your child. For example, hitting or yelling at other people is not a healthy way to express anger. Brainstorm what would be healthy options to express anger. Validate your child's feelings, while still holding them accountable for healthy behavior.

You don't have to have all the answers, but understanding and reassurance will go a long way.

© National Alliance for Grieving Children 2016

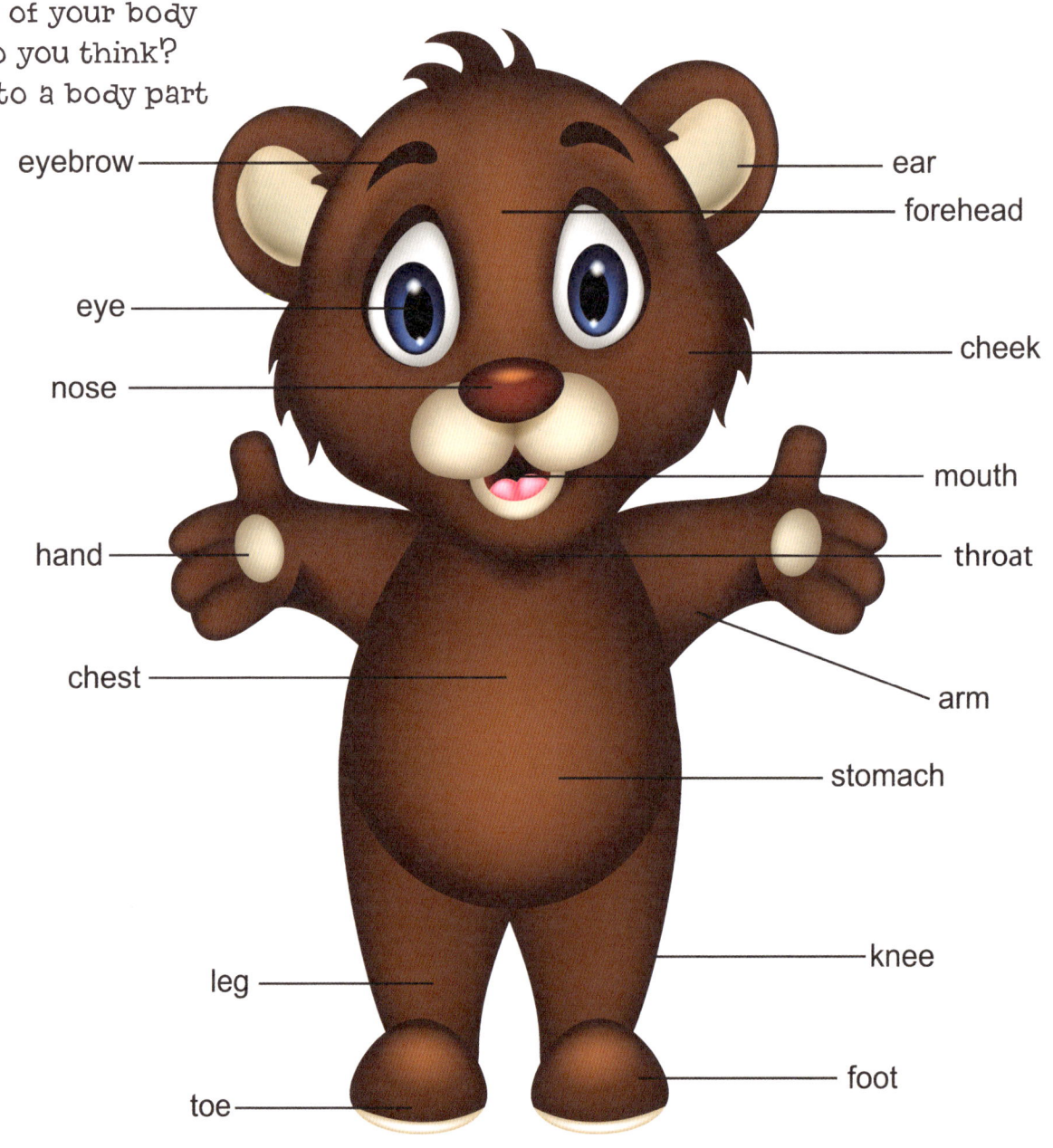

Parent Tip:
This activity provides a context to talk to your child about the connection between their feelings and their bodies.

Grief can manifest itself physically in children. Has your child been complaining of headaches or stomachaches? It could be related to their grief. If your child equates a particular feeling to a specific part of their body, you might explore this further with them.

A note of caution: Be careful to NOT read too much into this activity. Some children will just have fun drawing lines, and matching words with particular parts of the body.

Feelings are Physical

ACTIVITY TIME: What parts of your body do feelings affect? What do you think? Connect each feeling word to a body part

- Angry
- Loved
- Worried
- Happy
- Guilty
- Frustrated
- Annoyed
- Relieved
- Excited
- Anxious
- Overwhelmed
- Lonely
- Stressed

Labels on bear: eyebrow, ear, forehead, eye, cheek, nose, mouth, hand, throat, chest, arm, stomach, leg, knee, toe, foot

© National Alliance for Grieving Children 2016

26

Feelings Factory

Grief can generate a lot of strong feelings. It can be helpful to understand what feelings you are having and to be able to express those feelings in a safe way.

ACTIVITY TIME: Color in how much of each feeling you feel below. Is a "feeling explosion" brewing inside you?

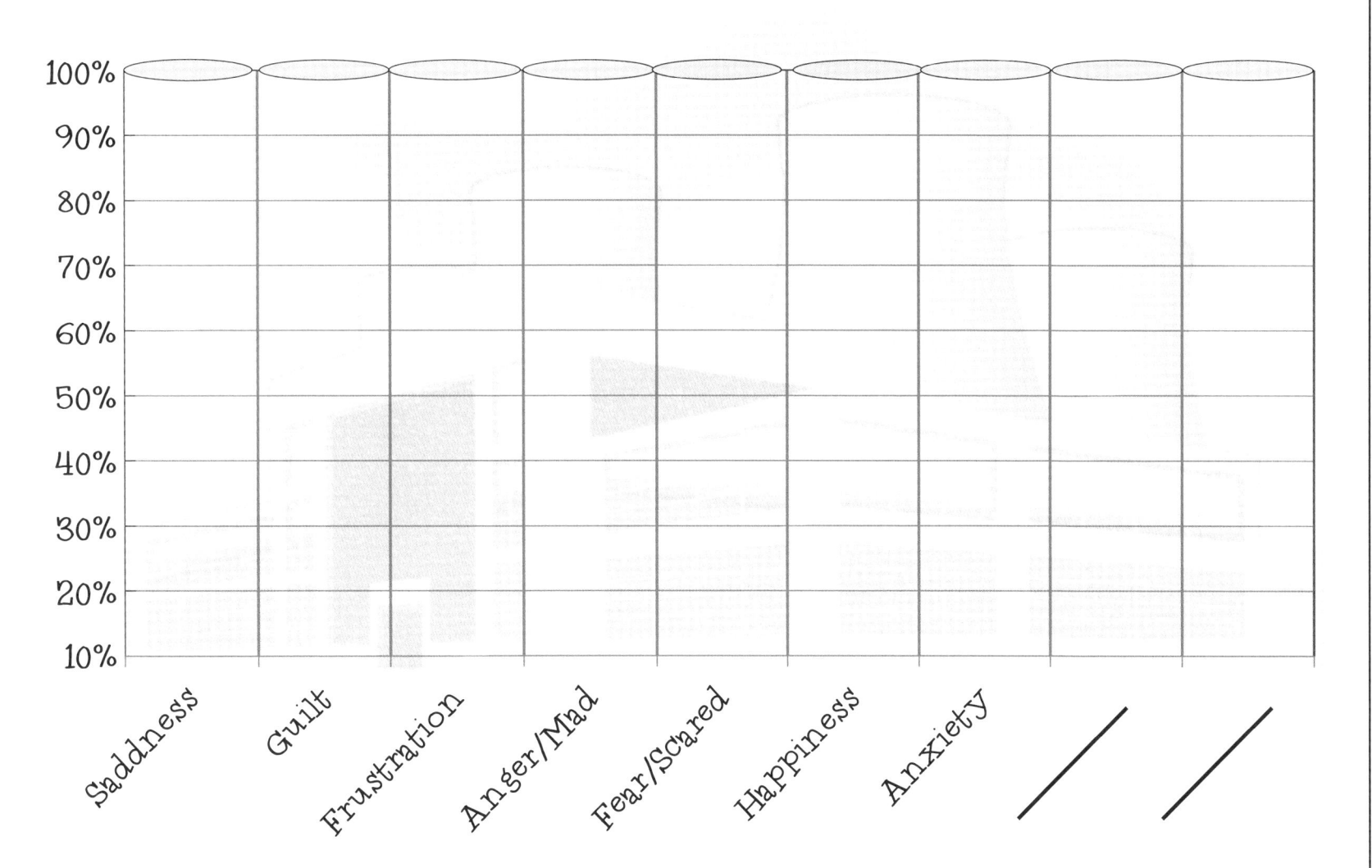

	Saddness	Guilt	Frustration	Anger/Mad	Fear/Scared	Happiness	Anxiety	/	/
100%									
90%									
80%									
70%									
60%									
50%									
40%									
30%									
20%									
10%									

Parent Tip:
Since grief changes over time, you can revisit this activity in order to "check in" with your child.

Grief is not a linear process. It is natural for grief to come in "waves" and intensify at times. Typically "grief flares" occur when there are other stressors like the beginning of a school year, holidays, and special days. They can also occur unexpectedly without a direct stressor.

Revisiting this activity will help both you and your child understand what they are feeling at the moment, allowing you to provide encouragement and support, and the opportunity for your child to make a plan about how to handle these often difficult feelings.

© National Alliance for Grieving Children 2016

Parent Tip:
It is natural for feelings of grief to "rise to the surface" at very unexpected times. Often times surprising feelings are triggered by events or things we encounter.

Though grief triggers can be unexpected, they can also become familiar over time.

The following activity provides the opportunity to identify the triggers your child has experienced.

Talk with them about their reaction when it happened and what they did to cope in the situation. It might help to anticipate some situations your child may face and rehearse with your child what they can do or say in that situation.

Grief is Full of Surprises

Grief is the reaction people have to loss. Grief can affect every part of a person's life! Grief can affect our thoughts, feelings, bodies, and relationships.

Also, there are a lot of things in our lives that might "trigger" our grief. A "grief trigger" is something that makes you think about your loss and may bring up a lot of feelings.

Some grief triggers can be expected such as approaching holidays or special days.

On the other hand, grief triggers can pop-up unexpectedly anywhere, anytime, which is what makes them so surprising.

Some examples of grief triggers:

- Having to explain that your person has died.

- Seeing someone who looks like your person.

- Seeing an object that belonged to your person.

- Tasting a favorite food of your person.

- Hearing a song that reminds you of them.

- Going somewhere that you used to go to together.

- Experiencing a new loss or disappointment.

© National Alliance for Grieving Children 2016

ACTIVITY TIME: Write about or draw a picture of times you have experienced "grief triggers".

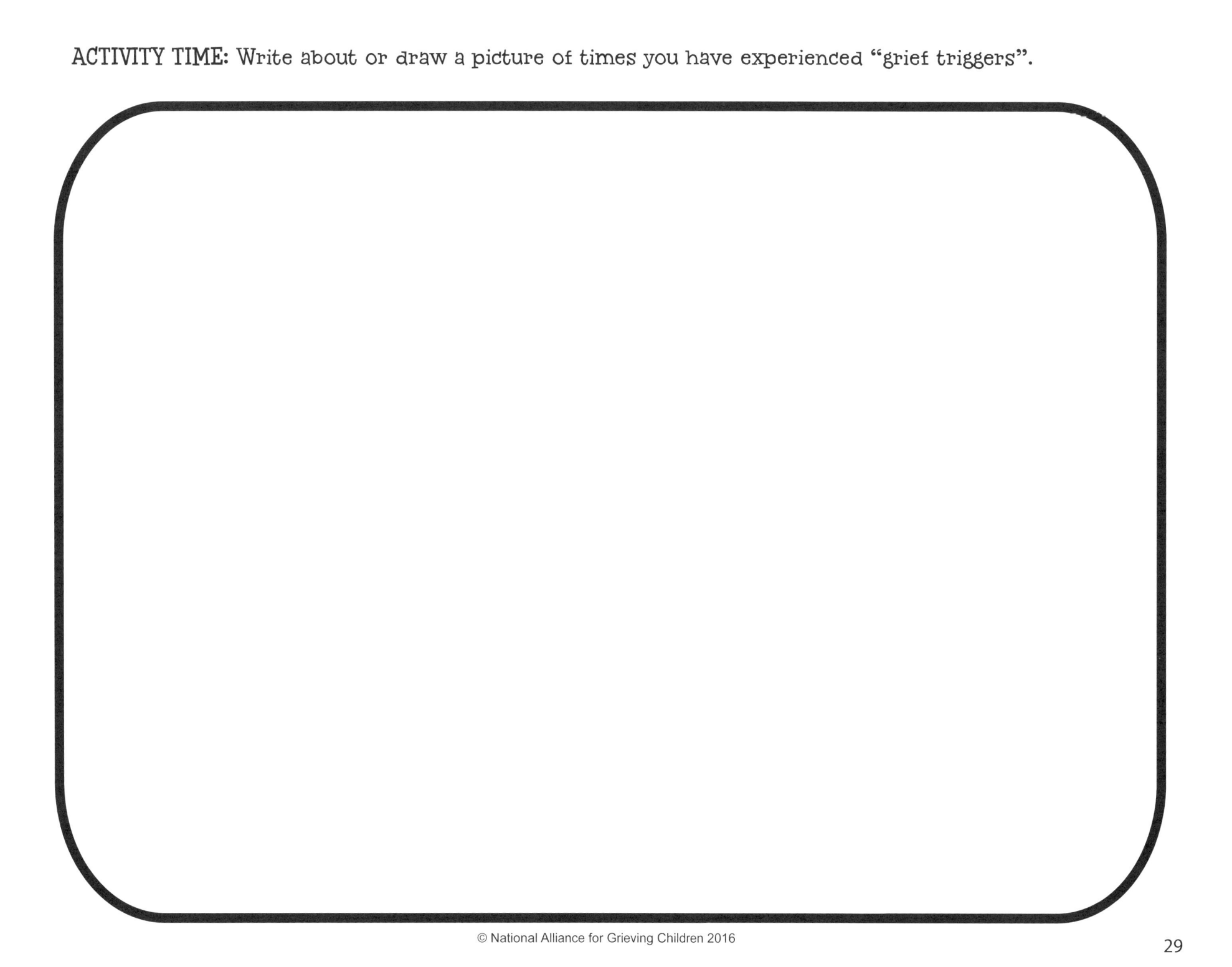

Parent Tip:
It is natural to experience a variety of moods and changes when grieving.

This activity provides a way to engage your child in conversation about the different moods they might have and what things might trigger these different moods.

You can use this opportunity to talk with your child about how to manage different moods, just like how we sometimes have to make the most out of rainy days.

Rainy Days Happen

Just like the weather, moods change. A mood is how a person feels on the inside, like sad, nervous, scared, or happy. You could be having a bunch of happy-go-lucky, fun, sunny days and then all of a sudden a dreary, rainy, feel-bad day can come along.

ACTIVITY TIME: (1) Draw a picture of something that makes you feel like a dreary, rainy, feel-bad day. (2) Next, draw what makes you feel better when you are in a "bad mood".

© National Alliance for Grieving Children 2016

ACTIVITY TIME: Use the circles below to draw faces that show the different moods you have experienced since your person died.

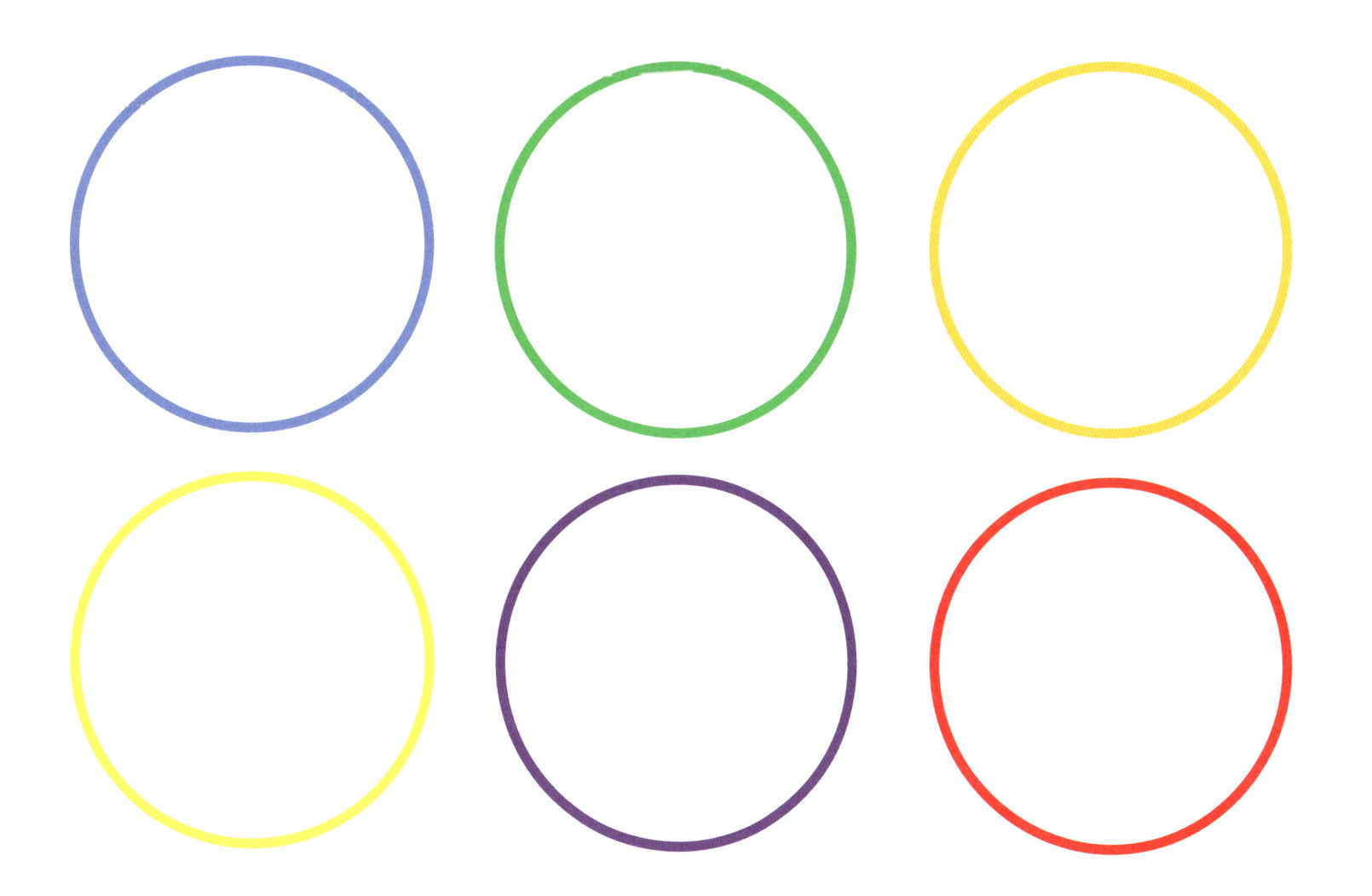

Parent Tip:
Younger children might find it easier to understand moods using this activity. It is a fun way to think about our different moods by giving our moods "faces." Ask them what moods they have from time to time. You can review the examples of moods provided if they are struggling and allow them to draw a face that represents that mood. You and your child can show each other these faces by making a fun game out of it. Make faces at each other representing different moods and try not to smile. The person who can do it the longest without smiling wins!

Some moods to choose from:

amused – angry – annoyed – ashamed – awkward – bittersweet – blah – bored – calm – cheerful – confused – cranky – depressed – disappointed – energetic – enraged – excited – exhausted – flirty – frustrated – giddy – gloomy – grateful – grumpy – happy – hopeful – indifferent – irritated – jealous – lazy – lonely – loved – mad – moody – nervous – numb – optimistic – peaceful – pessimistic – relaxed – restless – rushed – sad – satisfied – shocked – silly – sleepy – smart – sneaky – stressed – surprised – thankful – touched – uncomfortable – weird

© National Alliance for Grieving Children 2016

Parent Tip:
This is a good time to think about and talk about how grief can be difficult and encourage your child to let you know if he or she is having a difficult time.

Even if you have a good relationship with your child, it can be helpful for them to hear from you that they can talk to you about anything. This can create the safe space needed to reflect on the important changes they may be experiencing after the death of their person.

(Note: The solution for this maze is on page 78.)

The Twists & Turns of Grief

Grief can sometimes make people feel like they are "going crazy". Life can begin to feel unpredictable and that is hard! Like a maze, grief is full of twists, turns, and sometimes roadblocks. Just like a maze, you want to stay with it and you WILL find your way!

ACTIVITY TIME: Find your way through this maze, over and under the lines.

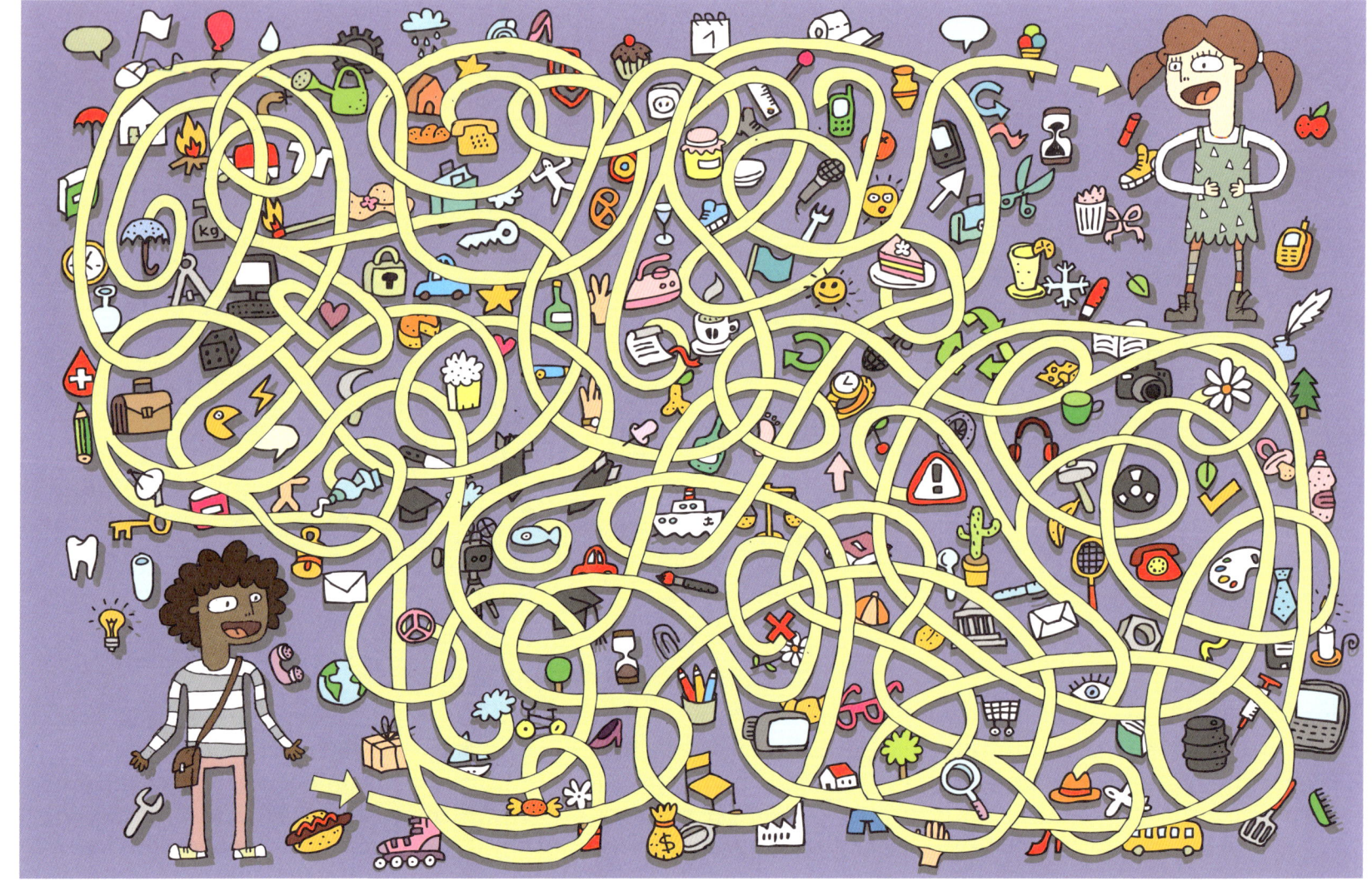

© National Alliance for Grieving Children 2016

My Support...
How I Cope with Grief

Parent Tip:

After someone dies it can sometimes be hard to have fun. This week plan time together as a family to enjoy some "fun time": go to a park, watch a movie, take a walk, or have a family game night. Take time to laugh and enjoy each other's company. It's okay to miss your person who died, but it's also okay to feel happy and keep living too.

After a family member's death, children often struggle to adapt to life without that person and to the absence of the role that person played in their lives and in their families.

Consider using this activity as an opportunity to reassure your child that you are still a family even though a significant person has died.

My Family

ACTIVITY TIME: Draw a picture of your family. Include some of the things you like to do together as a family.

I Am Supported

ACTIVITY TIME: Write about or draw all of the places you go (examples: home, school, church, family, friends, after school activities). For each place list the people who can support you in your grief.

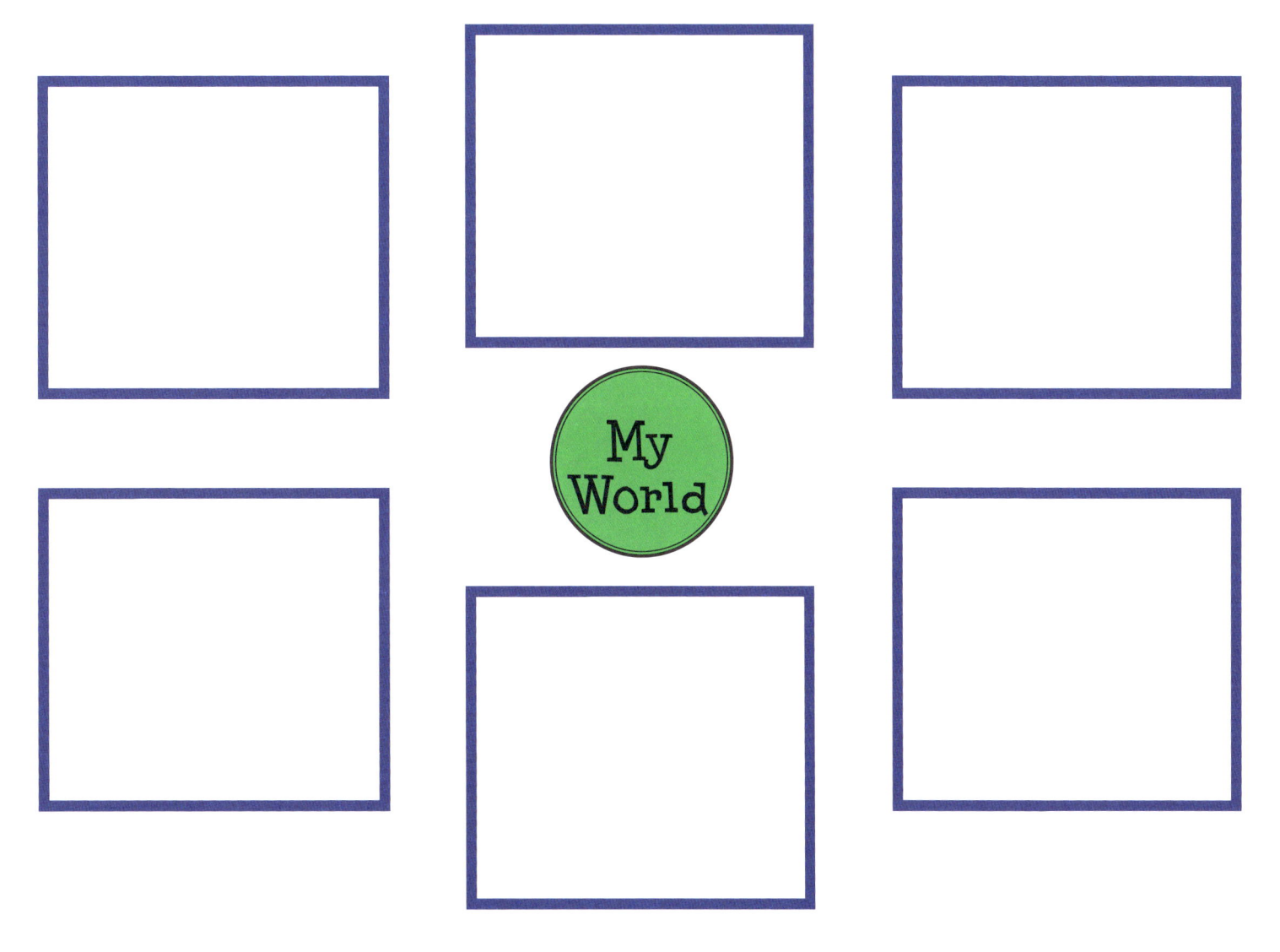

My World

Parent Tip:
Consider using this activity as an opportunity to discuss ways your child can access their support network. For example, make a list of telephone numbers and e-mail addresses they can use. You might also discuss what are appropriate ways to contact their support people. Be specific and set clear limits on technology use (For example: texting is only allowed to family members and is not allowed after 7p.m.).

This is a great way to reassure your child that they are not alone, while helping them to identify those "safe" people in their lives to reach out to when they might be having a difficult time.

© National Alliance for Grieving Children 2016

Parent Tip:

Hero stories and stories about ordinary people doing great things are a huge part of children's lives. Children will pretend to be their favorite characters, fighting off the "bad guys" and saving the day. This activity offers the opportunity to think about and talk about your child's innate strengths.

To be "brave" does not mean we are not scared, or sad, or angry. Being "brave" is finding ways to cope with these feelings in ways that are healthy, rather than in ways that might be hurtful. Think of other times your child has been brave and remind them of their previous struggles but eventual success.

I Am Brave

Do you know how brave you are? You CAN cope with difficult situations. Whether someone says something hurtful to you or you are just having a hard day, you are the superhero of your life story! Sometimes being brave means asking for help when you need it. Even superheroes have friends they call on for help! Are you brave enough to ask for help?

ACTIVITY TIME: Color in and personalize the superhero to look like you.

© National Alliance for Grieving Children 2016

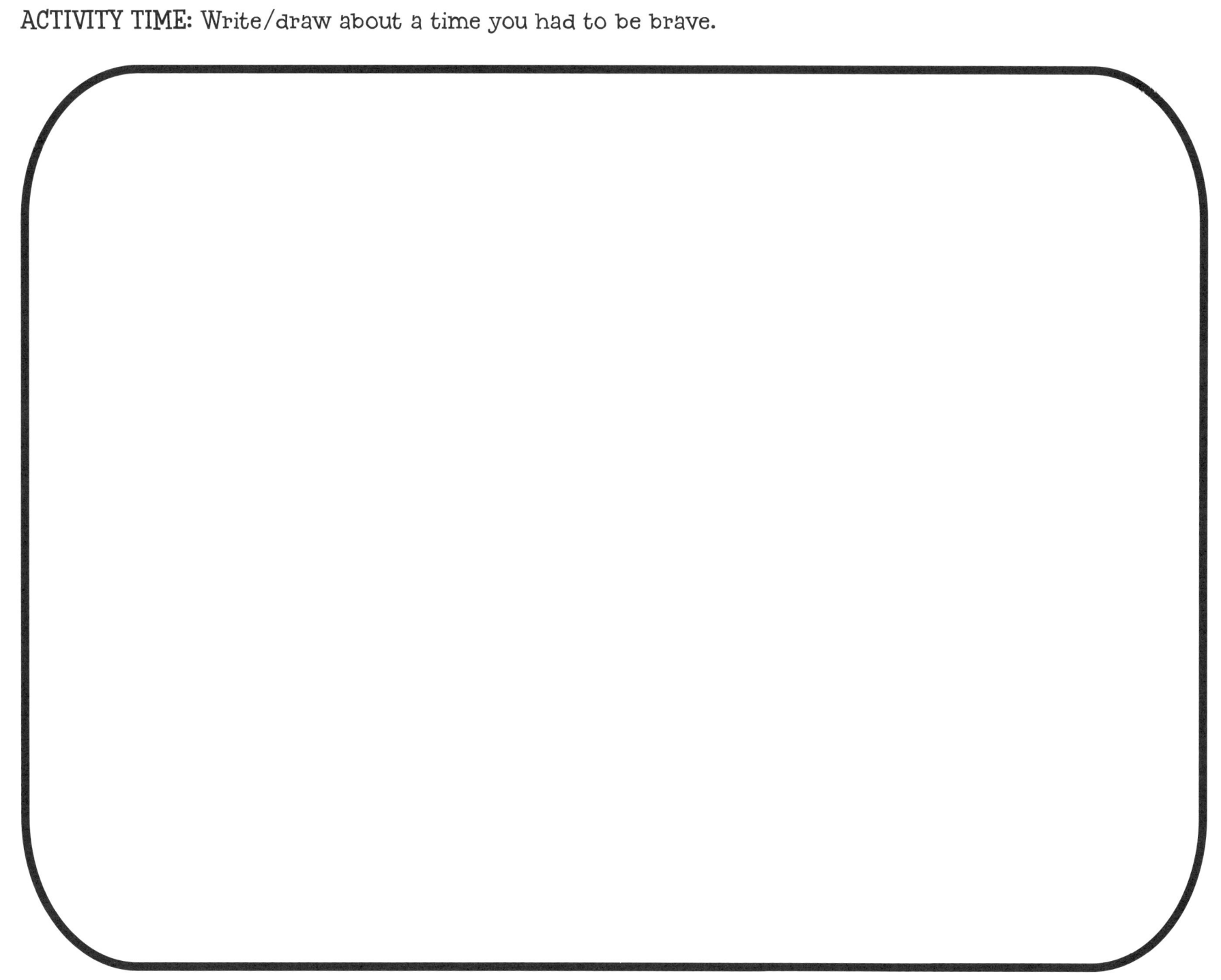

ACTIVITY TIME: Write/draw about a time you had to be brave.

Parent Tip:
The death of someone can impact many of one's daily routines. Your child's person played a specific role in their life and their death might have brought about a number of changes.

You and your child might grieve these changes. This is a normal part of adapting to new routines, and a new pace of life.

This activity can help you process some of these changes with your child and make plans for new routines.

All Kinds of Changes

The death of someone can bring all kinds of changes. What has changed in your life? **ACTIVITY TIME:** Write/Draw the changes that have happened in your life. Try to include both changes you dislike and changes you like.

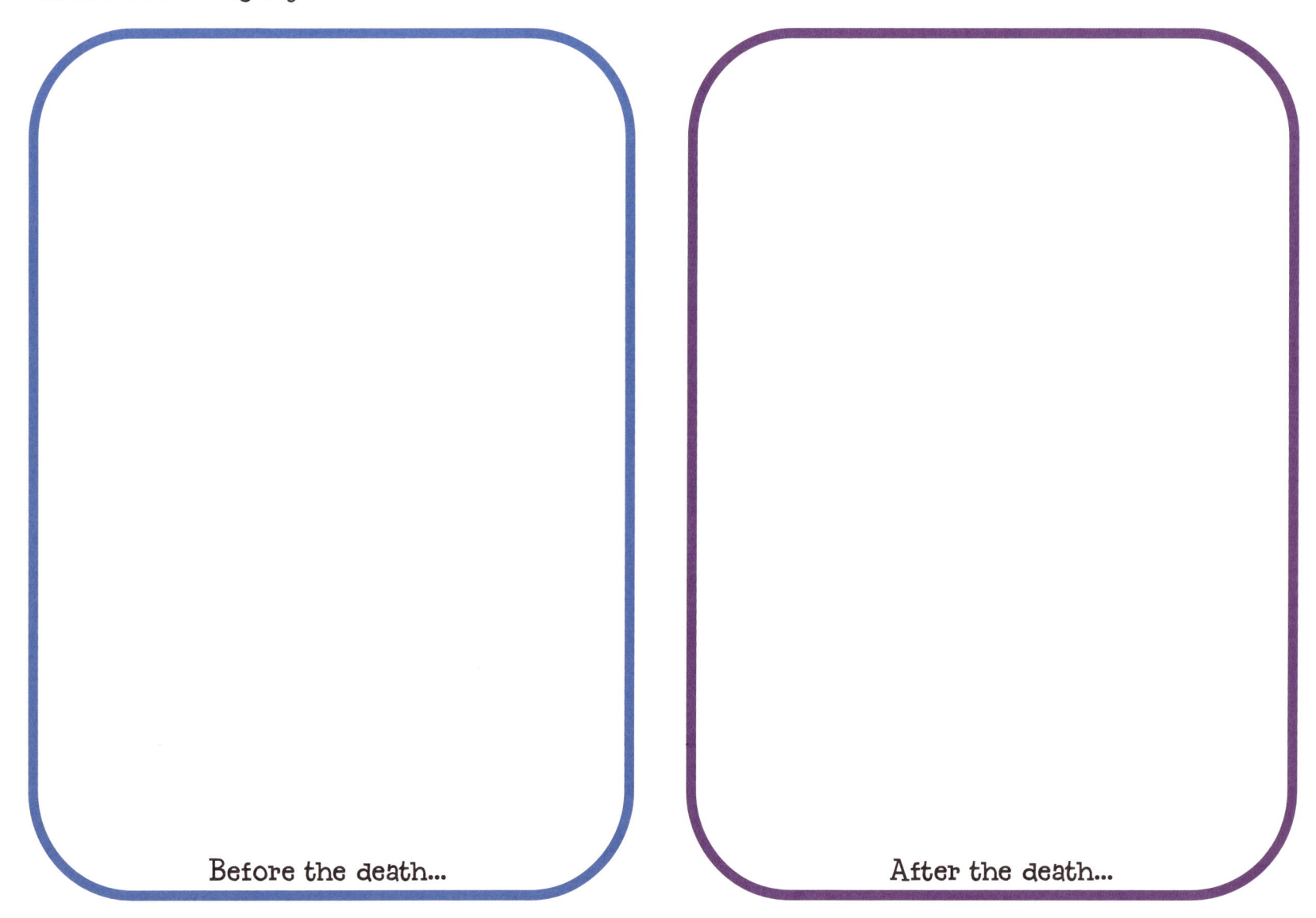

Before the death...

After the death...

© National Alliance for Grieving Children 2016

I Never, I Wonder, I Wish

It's natural to have feelings of regret and even guilt when someone dies. Those are big feelings.

After someone dies, people may wonder what life would be like if their person had not died or if they could have done something to prevent their person from dying. Some people may think about all the things they never got to say to or do with their person. Very often, people wish they had done something differently while their person was still alive, or just wish things could be different now. Have you ever felt this way before? When?

ACTIVITY TIME: Write or draw your responses.

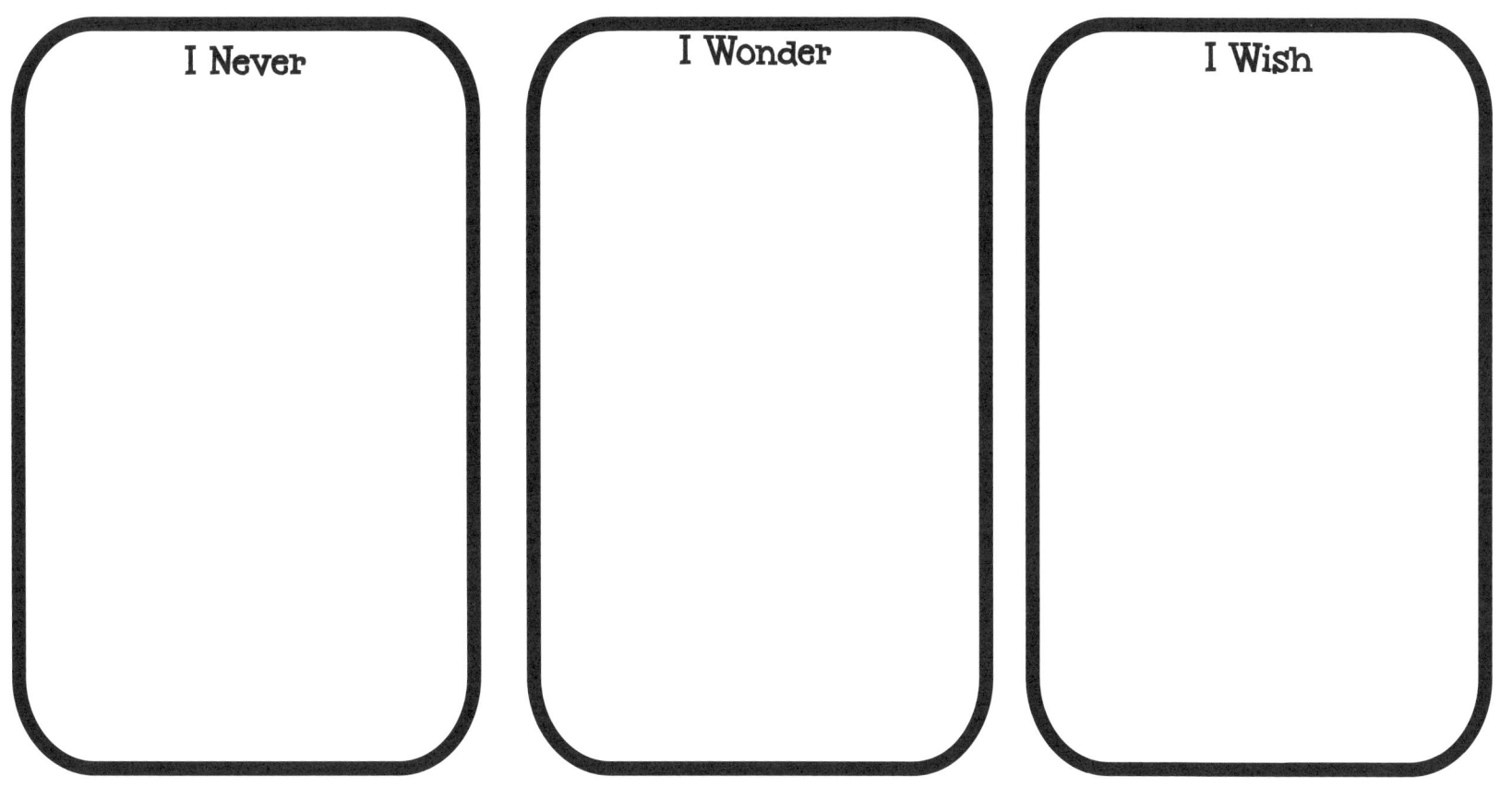

I Never	I Wonder	I Wish

Parent Tip:
It is natural for children to sometimes relate a person's death to something the children did or did not do. For example, sometimes children might think that if they had been better behaved their person would not have died.

This activity provides an opportunity for you to talk with your child about feelings of regret or guilt. It is okay for them to have the feelings they have, but you can also remind them that their person died for reasons unrelated to your child's thoughts and/or behaviors.

Be careful NOT to overwhelm your child, though, by telling them NOT to feel a particular way. Simply open up communication and provide encouragement to help them better understand the reality of what happened, rather than their interpretation of the circumstances.

© National Alliance for Grieving Children 2016

Parent Tip:

The next few pages provide an opportunity to reinforce the message to your child that grief has many different emotions, like sadness, anger, frustration, or fear. Emphasize that if they are experiencing any of these feelings, it is natural to do so.

If they are not experiencing any of these feelings, reassure them that everyone grieves in their own time and in their own way, and that it is alright if they are not feeling any of these feelings.

This page is a good time to talk about how a person can both feel sad and still be "okay". Being aware of feelings and coping with them in healthy ways is helpful as your child adapts to the absence of someone in their life.

It's Okay to Feel Sad

After a death, it is natural to feel sad. Just because someone has died, it does not mean that you will not miss them or want to see and talk with them. It is also natural to forget for a moment that they died.

The things you used to like to do may no longer seem fun anymore.

When you are having a sad moment, try to think of what would help. It might help to have a "good cry".

Sometimes, it might help to talk about or draw out how you are feeling. Other times, you may want to look through pictures or hear stories about your person who died.

Maybe having a warm meal or a rest could be what you need. Even though sadness is a feeling, it is a feeling that can make you feel very tired physically.

Be sure to take care of yourself!

© National Alliance for Grieving Children 2016

ACTIVITY TIME: Match the following comfort activity words to the correct pictures. Circle the ways you find comfort when you feel sad.

Cry   Talk   Comfort Food   Create   Remember   Rest

What other ways do YOU find comfort?

Parent Tip:
This page offers an opportunity for your child to think about ways to comfort themselves when they might be feelings sad. Think beyond the activities on this page, even, as you explore with your child how to deal with feelings of sadness.

You might want to share with your child the ways you comfort yourself when you are sad.

As mentioned previously, children love to hear stories from our lives. This includes stories about how to deal with life's difficulties. Stories provide a wonderful way to teach children important things about life without lecturing, or constantly correcting their behavior.

The stories shared also leave lasting impressions on children as they are developing their own ways of understanding the world.

© National Alliance for Grieving Children 2016

Parent Tip:
Anger is a natural reaction for some children when someone dies. It is okay for your child to feel mad. If you child is expressing anger over the death, affirm their experience by saying something like, "I see that you are angry – All of us feel angry at times."

Normalizing this feeling and providing your child with attention will often de-escalate their anger. It is also helpful to strategize with your child when they are not deep in their feelings of anger about how to calm themselves when they do feel angry.

We have included a simple calming exercise you can teach your child on the next page. This can serve as a helpful coping mechanism with a wide range of emotions, including anger.

It's Okay to Feel Mad

Angry or mad feelings want to "GET OUT"!!! Holding these feelings in may make you feel like you are going to explode!

An emotional explosion can lead to trouble, like breaking something or hurting someone. It's important to talk about your feelings with someone you trust and choose a positive way to express your anger. It is okay to feel mad. Anger just needs to be expressed it in a healthy way.

There are three guidelines to consider when getting your mad out.

Questions:
Can you think of a time when you got your mad out and you did follow these guidelines? What happened?

Can you think of a time when you got your mad out and did NOT follow these guidelines? What happened?

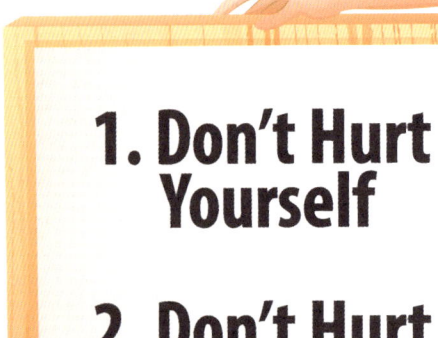

1. **Don't Hurt Yourself**
2. **Don't Hurt Others**
3. **Don't Destroy Property**

© National Alliance for Grieving Children 2016

Calming Exercise

Deep breathing can help a person calm down.

Step 1: Close your eyes and take a deep breath in - just like you are smelling beautiful flowers.

Step 2: Now blow all the air out - just like you are blowing out birthday candles.

ACTIVITY TIME: Color in the flowers and the candles. Keep breathing in and out a few times and see how your body feels. Next time you get upset remember this exercise to help calm your body down.

© National Alliance for Grieving Children 2016

Parent Tip:
There is a very physical component to fear. In fact, this is true of other feelings as well, i.e. sadness, anger, or frustration. This calming exercise teaches children a way to "calm" themselves in a very physical way.

Practice this exercise with your child. Teach them to take their time as they take a deep breath, breathing in the smell of their make-believe flowers, and then blowing out as if they are blowing out candles. Have your child repeat this exercise a few times.

Individuals who participate in this activity will often find themselves calming down and learn a new technique for coping with the difficult emotions that grief might bring.

Parent Tip:
Bedtime can often be a difficult time for children, in general. It can be especially difficult after a death.

Fears can be overwhelming for children. It's important to acknowledge that the fear they feel is real (even if what they are afraid of is unlikely) and help them to work on a way to calm themselves when they are afraid. (See the "Calming Exercise" page for an exercise your child can use when feeling anxious.)

It can be helpful for children to have a routine at bedtime: reading a story, sharing stories about your day, singing songs, or other meaningful activities.

Fear

Everyone feels scared once in a while, even adults. Lots of people are scared of spiders, monsters, heights, dying, losing a loved one or even the dark.

Night time can be especially scary. Sometimes having bad dreams or being scared makes going to sleep difficult.

PLEASE DO NOT FEED THE FEARS

What is something you are scared of?

Do you get scared at bed time? What are some things that scare you at night?

What is something you can do that helps you when you feel afraid?

Share with your family some things you are scared of and find out what they are scared of too.

© National Alliance for Grieving Children 2016

ACTIVITY TIME: Color the friendly monsters below and talk about your fears. Which fears do you think are more likely and which ones are less likely to happen?

Parent Tip:
This activity provides an opportunity to talk with your child about the many fears they might have.

Use this activity as a context to identify and discuss fears that are less likely to happen. This can help your child realize that they do not really need to worry about some of the fears they might have.

Be sure NOT to down play their fears, but use this as a time to acknowledge them and provide a safe space to explore the reality of their impact on your child.

You can also relate back to the "brave" activity and talk about ways to cope.

© National Alliance for Grieving Children 2016

45

Parent Tip:
Sometimes children have a difficult time understanding why they are afraid. When asked why, they might simply answer, "because it's dark," or "I'm scared of the closet." You can help your child by further exploring what might be scary to them about these things. This will help "shed a light on their fears." This will open up the opportunity to talk with them about fears that are "real" and fears that are "not real."

Remember to validate their feelings and avoid too much lecturing. Focus on the "what helps" part of this activity as you help your child learn ways to calm themselves and cope.

Bringing Fears to Light

If you were in a dark room and it scared you, what would you do?

You could turn on the light, so you could see if something were really there. "Shining a light on" (or talking about) scary things might help make them a little less scary.

If something scary were to really happen, how would you react? What would happen next?

Do you remember when you made a list of support people? Look back at that. Do you think these people could help you when you are scared? How could they help?

ACTIVITY TIME: Write down one of your fears and what helps you when you are feeling scared.

MY FEAR:

WHAT HELPS:

© National Alliance for Grieving Children 2016

Big Energy Activities

ACTIVITY TIME: Circle the ways you would like to get your big energy out.

Rip up an old phone book or newspaper
(recycle the pages when you are done)

Wrestle with a pillow

Draw/Scribble on paper

Snowball or Water Balloon Fight!

Play a sport! Get your body moving!

What would you add?

Parent Tip:
Children, at times, may have a need to release extra energy. Children who are grieving are no different. But, uncontrolled release of energy, can sometimes be destructive, and even if let out in a healthy way, can still be messy. So, it is important that your child is responsible for the consequences of releasing this extra energy. Be sure to include your child in the clean-up after engaging in any "big energy" activities. It is important your child is responsible for the consequences of releasing this extra energy.

Some examples of "big energy" activities you might suggest to your child might be: tearing up the pages of an old phone book or wrestling with their pillow. This page provides some examples of things they could do to release big energy. The safety rules from earlier also apply to releasing extra energy.

© National Alliance for Grieving Children 2016

Parent Tip:
There may be some concern about offering children the opportunity to think about things they don't like in their lives.

Many kids express relief and gratitude when they're asked about topics or experiences most people are afraid to ask about. This activity doesn't force a child to come up with something they dislike, but allows them the opportunity to reflect on those things that might be a reality for them at the time.

If your child does not identify things they do not like, move on to the next activity. If they do identify something they do not like, do not over interpret what they are sharing or take it personally. Often the opportunity to express their frustrations is healing in and of itself.

What I Like & Dislike

Everyone has things in their life that they like and dislike. After someone dies things change and what we like or dislike might also change. You may have more chores now or get to go to the park less since someone has died.

ACTIVITY TIME: Write about or draw some of the things you like and dislike in your life.

What I **LIKE** in my life.

What I **DISLIKE** in my life.

© National Alliance for Grieving Children 2016

Grief At School and With Friends

Parent Tip:
If you feel comfortable take some time to sit down with someone from your child's school (like your child's teacher, counselor or principal) and discuss your situation. Explain to them how your child is doing and some struggles that he/she might be dealing with.

Brainstorm on ways that your child's school can help your child during this process.

For example: work out a way with your child and your child's teacher for your child to communicate with the teacher if they are struggling. All together, create a plan of action on how your child can regroup and then rejoin the class.

Grief at School

During the school year, most of your day will take place in school. It makes sense that you might feel grief at school.

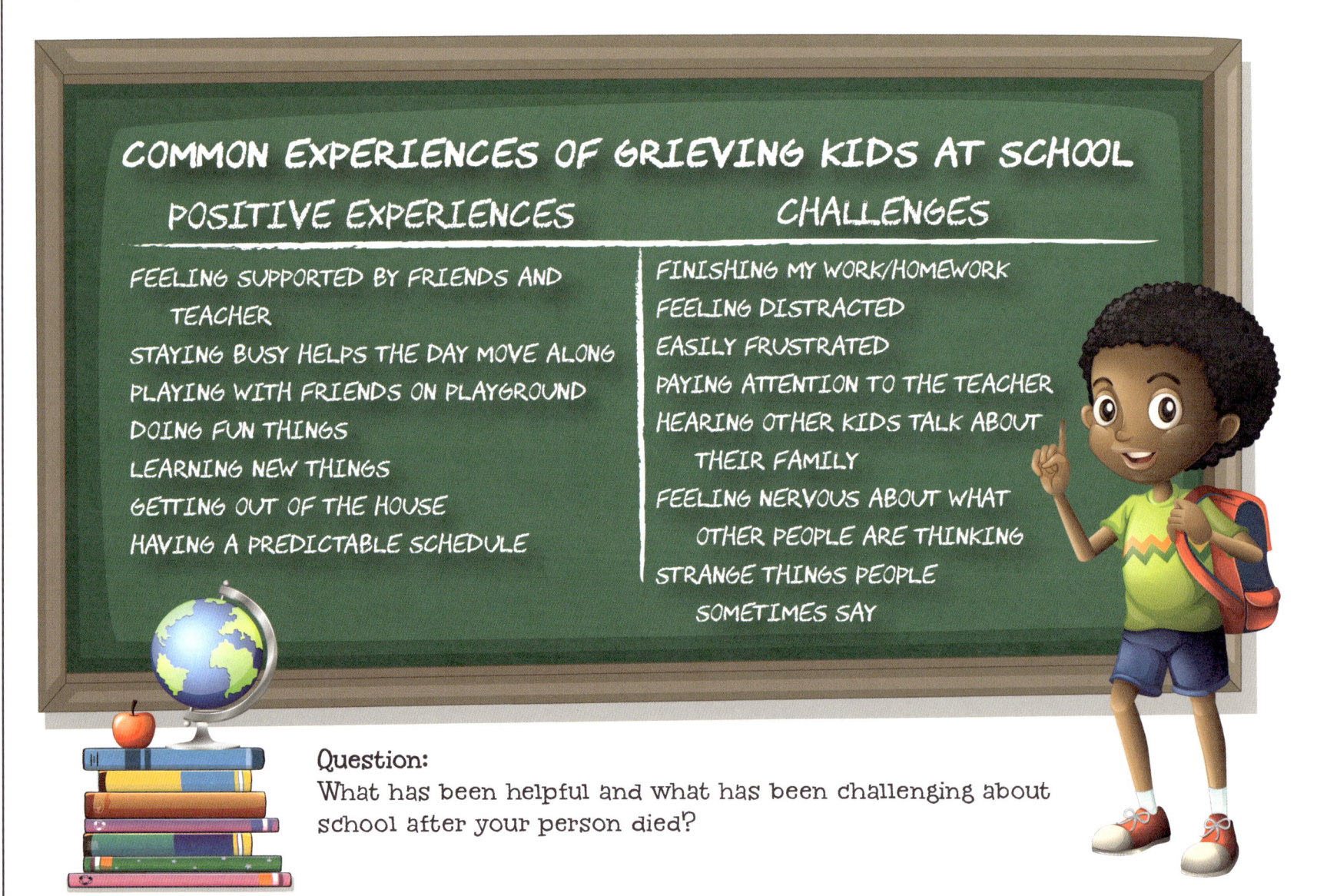

COMMON EXPERIENCES OF GRIEVING KIDS AT SCHOOL

POSITIVE EXPERIENCES
- FEELING SUPPORTED BY FRIENDS AND TEACHER
- STAYING BUSY HELPS THE DAY MOVE ALONG
- PLAYING WITH FRIENDS ON PLAYGROUND
- DOING FUN THINGS
- LEARNING NEW THINGS
- GETTING OUT OF THE HOUSE
- HAVING A PREDICTABLE SCHEDULE

CHALLENGES
- FINISHING MY WORK/HOMEWORK
- FEELING DISTRACTED
- EASILY FRUSTRATED
- PAYING ATTENTION TO THE TEACHER
- HEARING OTHER KIDS TALK ABOUT THEIR FAMILY
- FEELING NERVOUS ABOUT WHAT OTHER PEOPLE ARE THINKING
- STRANGE THINGS PEOPLE SOMETIMES SAY

Question:
What has been helpful and what has been challenging about school after your person died?

© National Alliance for Grieving Children 2016

What School Is Like for Me

ACTIVITY TIME: Draw a picture or write about how school helps you and how it challenges you.

Parent Tip:
There are all sorts of messages one receives from others after someone dies. Many are well meaning, but might actually have the opposite effect.

Has your child been given messages that are hurtful? In the case of the death of a parent, well-meaning adults around children may tell them they are now "the men/women of the house" and it will be their job to take care of the remaining parent.

Children should be allowed to remain children after a death. The suggestion they should now take the place of the deceased can dramatically add to children's stress and grief.

Hurtful Words

ACTIVITY TIME: Discuss some of the statements listed and share how you feel about hearing them. Write down some things you think would be hurtful to hear. Have any of these hurtful words ever been said to you?

- CRYING IS FOR BABIES
- JUST MOVE ON
- GET OVER IT!
- STOP BEING SO SAD!

© National Alliance for Grieving Children 2016

Responding to Hurtful Words

Sometimes we don't always hear what we want from others. People can say and do things which can feel hurtful. Sometimes, people may want to be helpful but say or do something hurtful because they just don't know how to help.

When this happens:
- Learn to be patient.
- Don't make it personal.
- It's okay to correct someone. Tell them what you need to hear.
- Tell someone you trust about the things you've heard that are hurtful.

Sometimes, kids may be hurtful on purpose. In these cases, you may need to make a plan to stop them from bullying you. You can ask yourself or tell someone:

1. What happened?
2. How would you like it to be different?
3. What things can you do to achieve your goal. (Who can help you? Remember the people in your support system.)
4. Choose your best option and take action. If your first plan does not work, go back through the steps, revise your plan, and try again.

Step 1: Get the Facts (Who, What, When, Where, How)

Step 2: Decide What You Want to be Different

Step 3: Brainstorm Your Options (Include Others Who Can Help You)

Step 4: Take Action (Change Plan as Needed)

© National Alliance for Grieving Children 2016

Parent Tip:
It can be hard for other young children to know the right thing to say to a grieving child. It can be equally difficult for a grieving child to be confident enough to inform others what they need to hear in order to feel supported.

Practice with your child what to say or how to act when someone says something hurtful.

Helpful Words

ACTIVITY TIME: Write down things you have heard that have been helpful to you or write down some of the things you would like to hear from your friends and other adults.

- I am here for you.
- Is there some way I can help?
- You can talk to me anytime.

What Comforts You?

Everyone likes to feel comfortable. But sometimes we have to work to feel comfort. When you are having a rough day what are the things you like to do to comfort yourself? Maybe wrap up in a blanket and watch your favorite movie or spend time with your best friend? Have you ever thought of what comfort feels like, tastes like, or sounds like?

Some people may think comfort feels like a warm hug, the first day of spring, or having lots of energy.
What does Comfort feel like to you?

Some people may think comfort tastes like Marshmallows, ices cream, chocolate, or a snow cone.
What does Comfort taste like to you?

Some people may think comfort sounds like a stream, walkes on the sand, music, or the quiet.
What does Comfort sound like to you?

Some people think if comfort could speak it would say everything will be ok. You can do it, I'm here for you.
If Comfort could talk, what would it say to you?

© National Alliance for Grieving Children 2016

Use this space to draw anything you want about the person who died.

Special Days and Remembering My Person

Parent Tip:
Special days and holidays can be difficult, especially in the first year. As a family, have a conversation about those days you consider special. Since you know those days might be difficult, take some time and plan how you as a family would like to mark the day, even if your plan is to do nothing.

There's no way to predict how you or your child will feel that day. Be flexible and patient with yourselves. Consider asking for help from your support system on those emotionally charged days.

Special Days & Holidays

The calendar year is full of special days that may remind you of the person who died. Birthdays, school events, valentine's day, mother's day, father's day, last day of school, first day of school, memorial day, Thanksgiving...

Any day where you WOULD have been with your person had they not died can bring up strong feelings.

ACTIVITY TIME: Draw or list some of the days that are special to you. Why are these days special? What did you do as a family or what did your person do to make these days special?

© National Alliance for Grieving Children 2016

ACTIVITY TIME: Do you have a favorite meal that is served on holidays or special days? Draw a picture of your favorite foods below.

Parent Tip:
Meals and food can play such an important part of many special days and celebrations. Children will often relate their favorite foods with these special occasions.

This activity offers a context to talk with your child about some of their favorite memories associated with the special days and celebrations in their life.

© National Alliance for Grieving Children 2016

Parent Tip:
Everyone has their own way of grieving. The same is true of remembering people who have died.

This activity offers the opportunity for you to reflect with your child about ways you can remember your person who has died. You can help your child by offering ideas about ways to remember, and even honor the memory of their person.

Remembering...My Way

There are many ways to remember a person who has died on special days. You could make their favorite food, draw a picture of them, visit their grave, write a letter or card to them, look at photographs, visit their favorite place, or do something positive for someone else in their honor.

ACTIVITY TIME: List or draw some of the ways that you can remember your person?

© National Alliance for Grieving Children 2016

Remembering...As a Family

Some families may make new traditions, participate in rituals and/or engage in activities to remember their person who died. Does your family do something together to remember your person?

ACTIVITY TIME: List/draw some of the ways as a family you can remember your person.

Parent Tip:
While everyone has their own way of remembering a person, shared activities as a family can provide an important context for connection, support, and encouragement.

This activity offers the opportunity to plan some ways you might remember as a family.

An activity you might consider doing with your child is to volunteer with a local charity in honor of their person who died. This can be a way to build strong bonds with your child, while honoring the memory of your person.

Parent Tip:
Sometimes children might have things they would like to say to the person who has died. The reality is that though a person has died, the relationship with them has not. Children will often think about the person, or even talk to the person in their own thoughts and mind. This activity provides a concrete way for children to express things to their person that they might be feeling or thinking.

For younger children, you may want to help them by writing what they tell you to write. Use the writing prompts to help with structuring the letter.

This is also a good time to talk about how people who have died can live on through a person's memories.

A Letter to Your Person

Imagine you could send a letter to your person who died. What would you want to say to them?

ACTIVITY TIME: On the next page, write a letter to your person who died.
Use any of the prompts (in any order) on this page to get started.

Writing Prompts:

Dear (Name of Your Person Who Died),
I want to let you know…
I am sorry…
I never..
I think about…
I hope you know…
My life these days is…
You helped me…
I think of you when…
I miss…
I really need…
Before you died, I wish I told you…
I've learned…
I remember the time we…
I hope…

From/Love, (Your name)

Optional Discussion Questions After Writing the Letter to Your Person:

1. Was it easy or difficult to write this letter?
2. Do you feel the letter contained what you wanted to say to your person who died?
3. Did the letter remind you of anything that you have not thought of lately?
4. Has this letter changed any way how you have been thinking about your grief?
5. Is there anything you would like to do with your letter?

© National Alliance for Grieving Children 2016

A Letter from Your Person to You

Parent Tip:
Even though a person is no longer physically present, they live on through memories. This is an exercise in connecting with the memory of the person who died, connecting with their "voice" and imagining what the person might say if they could write a letter.

Be sure to allow your child to express themselves in their own words. Children will often give voice to the things they need to hear from their person at the time, rather than what an adult in their life may think they need to hear.

Better understanding of what a child's needs comes when they are allowed to express their own thoughts and feelings.

Imagine if your person who died could send a letter to YOU.

What do you think they would want to say to you?

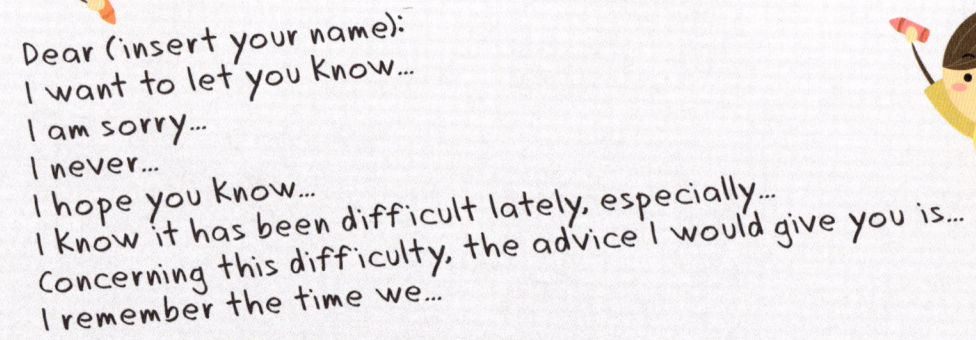

Dear (insert your name):
I want to let you know...
I am sorry...
I never...
I hope you know...
I know it has been difficult lately, especially...
Concerning this difficulty, the advice I would give you is...
I remember the time we...
I miss...
I am so proud of you, especially...
The one thing I wish I told you before I died is...
I've learned...
I really want you to know that...
It is okay to...
What I want for you is...
Don't forget...

From/With love,
(name of your person who died)

Optional Discussion Questions After Writing the Letter from your person to You:
1. Was it easy or difficult to write this letter?
2. Do you feel the letter captured your loved one's "voice"? What was it like for you to connect with their "voice"?
3. Did the letter remind you of anything that you have not thought of lately?
4. Was there anything that was written that surprises or impacts you? What is it? How does it affect you?
5. Has this experience changed any way you have been thinking about your grief?

ACTIVITY TIME: On the next page, write a letter to you from your person who died. Use any of the prompts (in any order) on this page to get started.

© National Alliance for Grieving Children 2016

Parent Tip:
This activity provides a fun way to create a make-believe adventure and relate it to the challenges of grief. Children often express their grief, through their play. Have fun with this activity. It is alright if they do not make all the metaphorical "connections" with their grief. It is perfectly okay if they simply have fun drawing a map and creating an adventure.

A Map of Grief

ACTIVITY TIME: On the next page, label the map of grief however you like. Do you think any of the following are a part of YOUR map of YOUR grief?

Volcano of Anger
Mountains of Regret
Waterfalls of Hope
Sea of Tears
Desert of Emptiness
Island of Loneliness
Swamp of Confusion
Field of New Beginnings
Great Fog of Forgetting

Evergreens of Envy
Waves of Emotion
Gulf of Separation
Bay of Peace
Sea of Silence
Whirlpool of Chaos
Sea of Memories
Treasure Trove of Memories

© National Alliance for Grieving Children 2016

© National Alliance for Grieving Children 2016

67

Use this space to draw anything you want.

A Year in Review

ACTIVITY TIME: Reflect on this past year. What are the things that have changed? How have you changed? Write about or draw a picture about the challenges you have faced this past year and the ways you have overcome or coped with these challenges.

Parent Tip:
Reflecting back can provide great insight while moving forward in life. There is much you can learn from the past year about the struggles you and your child might have had and the ways you overcame or coped with these challenges.

Allow your child to reflect on their own ideas about this past year, and share with them your perspective about this past year as well. You might even recall events from the past year as stories. These can become teachable moments that your child will remember for a long time.

Parent Tip:
This activity provides a fun way to talk about some very difficult things. Be sure not to "push" too hard, but allow your child to share as much or as little as they would like as part of this game. This is also a good activity to come back to from time-to-time to "check in" with each other and talk about how you are doing.

Consider adding your own questions to the game to tailor it to your family.

Game Time!

ACTIVITY TIME: It's time to play! Bring your own game pieces and begin at the ⊙. Pick any color category and question to get started. Once you answer a question, move forward the number of spaces your question is "worth". When you land on a new color, you get to choose which question to answer in that category.

GREEN	BLUE	RED
If you were an animal, what would you be and why? **MOVE+1**	Name three things you can do when you miss your person who died. **MOVE+1**	Name three good ways to help yourself when you feel angry **MOVE+1**
If you had a super power, what would you want it to be and what would you do with it? **MOVE+2**	Finish this sentence: When I feel sad I like to... **MOVE+1**	If you could take back one thing you said or did in your life, what would it be? **MOVE+2**
Which character from television or from a movie are you like? How are you like them? **MOVE+2**	Talk about a time you were recently sad. **MOVE+2**	Finish this sentence: I get angry when... **MOVE+2**
What is something you are looking forward to? **MOVE+3**	What is your grief like today? **MOVE+3**	Talk about the last time you felt very angry. **MOVE+3**
If you could travel anywhere, where would you go? Who would you want to go with you? **MOVE+3**	What advice would you give to a friend who had someone in their life die? **MOVE+3**	Talk about a time you had to be brave. **MOVE+3**

PURPLE	YELLOW	PINK (⊙)
What is one quality that you value in a friend? **MOVE+1**	What is your favorite activity we do as a family? **MOVE+1**	Finish this sentence: this week I struggled with... **MOVE+5**
What is a "grief trigger". Give an example from your life. **MOVE+2**	Talk about something nice you have recently done for someone else. **MOVE+2**	What is one thing that you think you could change to make yourself happier? **MOVE+5**
Name two safe places you can go when you feel scared. **MOVE+2**	Finish this sentence: I am proud of... **MOVE+2**	Finish this sentence: I hope... **MOVE+5**
When was you grief last "triggered"? Talk about it. **MOVE+3**	Name three people who support you. **MOVE+3**	Name three feelings you felt today. **MOVE+5**
Finish this sentence: I worry about... **MOVE+3**	Finish this sentence: I feel supported by my family when... **MOVE+3**	What is a favorite memory of your person who died? **MOVE+5**

© National Alliance for Grieving Children 2016

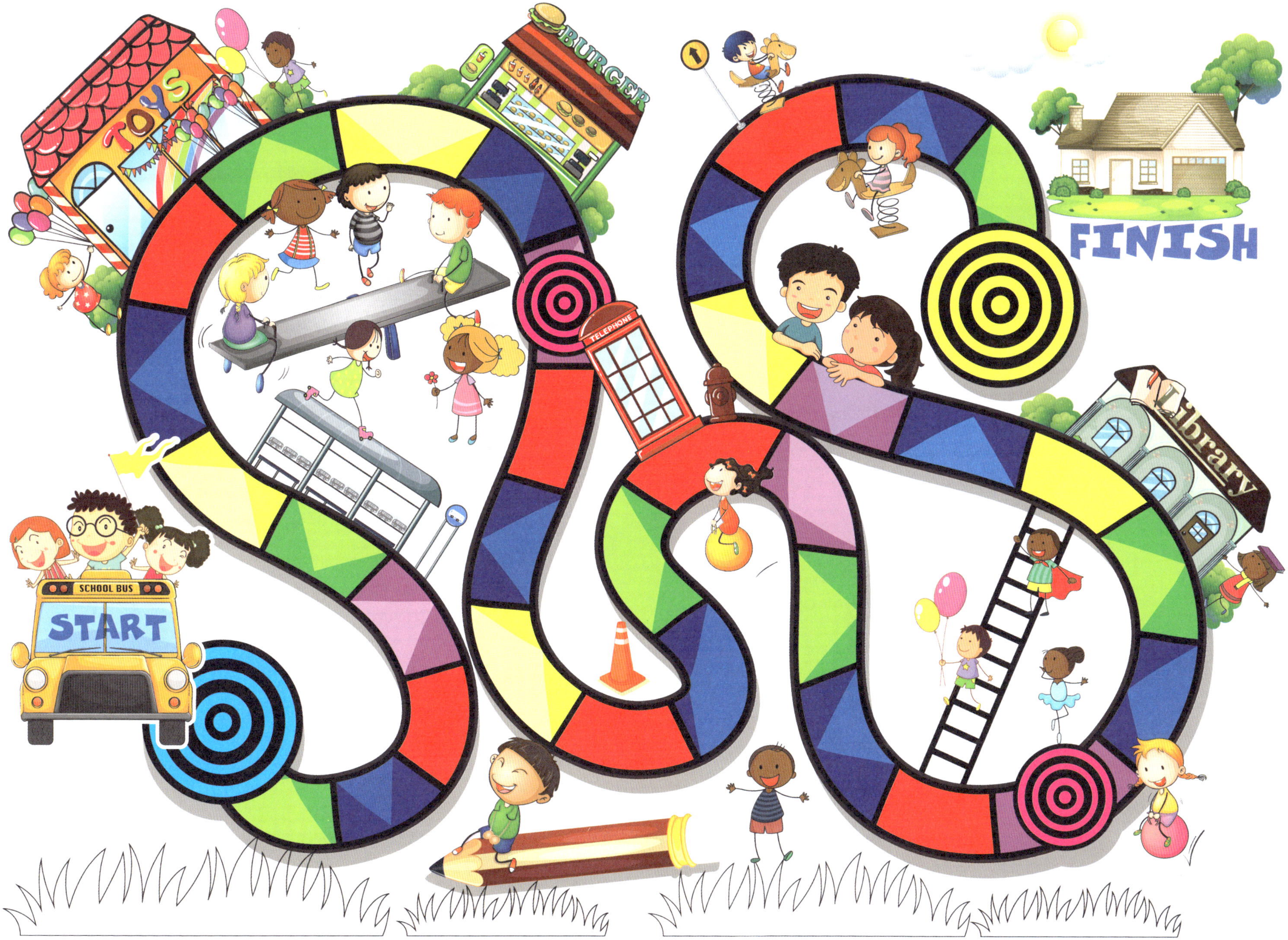
TOYS
BURGER
FINISH
TELEPHONE
Library
SCHOOL BUS
START

Closing Message to Kids

The death of someone in your life has a lasting impact. If you have completed all the activities in this book, it does not mean that you will not continue to miss your person, or have feelings of grief.

We hope you will remember the activities you completed and the things you learned from this book.

We would encourage you to use these activities again in the future when you feel the need to remember, reflect, be encouraged, and learn. Most of the activities in this book can be completed on a separate sheet of paper by simply following the instructions and the information can be re-read over and over again.

We wish you all the best as you continue to grow and to live each day. When you feel alone, remember the people you have identified that are part of your support system and reach out to them. When you are feeling the many feelings of grief, remember that it is natural to experience all kinds of emotions. Remember the things you identified in this book that can help you cope with your feelings.

Lastly, remember that you can be okay and still grieve.

Closing Message to Parents/Caregivers Raising Bereaved Children:

We hope the activities and information in this book have been helpful to you and your child. The purpose of this book is to help create a space where children can normalize their feelings of grief, remember their person who has died, identify their own strengths and support system around them, and connect with their parent or caregiver around the topic of grief.

Completing this book does not mean the end of your child's grief. Grief is not a problem we are trying to solve, it is an experience we live. It is natural for children to revisit their grief at different times throughout their lives, even into adulthood.

It is our hope that the coping skills and insights they have gained through this book will continue to assist them with the ebbs and flows of life. Remember, the encouragement, support, and nurturing from you and the other loving adults in their lives are the most important factors in a child's mental, emotional, physical, and spiritual health as they continue to adapt to their loss.

Common Questions from Parents/Caregivers Raising Bereaved Children:

How do I tell my child that someone has died?
Staff at the Dougy Center

Telling a child that their father or mother, sister or brother has died ranks among the most difficult tasks a parent will encounter. There is no "one size fits all" in terms of what to say, but there are a few general principles that may help. The explanation you offer your children will vary depending on the circumstances of the family member's death; was there an acute or long term illness, or did the death occur suddenly and without warning? In either case, it is important to talk to your children as soon as possible after the death. Start simply and honestly, and preferably in person, by saying something like, "I have some sad news to share with you. Today your Dad was in a car accident. The ambulance took him to the hospital but he was hurt too badly and he died." First and foremost, be honest and avoid any temptation to alter the truth. If there are questions you can't answer, say, "I don't know, but I can try to find out." You may want to wait and see what questions your children have before giving more information than they can handle at one time. It's also helpful to reassure them that, "this is hard, but we will get through it together."

What do I tell my child if their person died from suicide?
Pamela Gabbay, M.A., FT

When talking with your child, it is important to take into consideration your child's age. Younger children often process information in bite size pieces. Older children and teens often have complex questions and might want a lot of information. When deciding how much to tell your child, follow their lead based on the questions that you're being asked. Answering children's questions honestly is important. So is explaining suicide in terms that they can understand. For example, "Your mom died of suicide." Suicide means that a person caused their own death. As a parent, you might be hesitant to say these words, but children often overhear the word suicide and might be confused by what it means. By having this open conversation, you are allowing your child the opportunity to ask questions and have concerns addressed. Children will often ask "why." It is okay to say, "I don't know" if you don't know why. If you have been struggling with how to have these conversations, or have not been fully honest up to this point, try not to be too hard on yourself. After all, you are also grappling with your own grief and sorrow. Going forward, the key is to create an environment where difficult, yet necessary, conversations can take place.

What do I tell my child if their person died from homicide?
Alesia Alexander, MSW, LCSW, CT, Comfort Zone Camp
As in most "grief talks" or "how do I break bad news" questions, timing is everything. In the case of a loss due to homicide, this is even more central to supporting your young person and family. The very nature of a homicide involves urgency and quick responses by support and law enforcement personnel that may involve participating in an open investigation, or an "in the moment" or "on the scene" media presence that the family or child/teen may be involved in before any real talk or support can be given. Supporters should be alert and very sensitive to whether or not the child/teen was a witness to any events preceding the death, or the actual event itself before attempting to talk with the child/teen. This awareness can help you garner responses and resources for addressing possible trauma or other related issues present. Support offered should factor in any need a child or teen may have about what they have seen or heard about their person on TV or other social media. Information shared should seek to clarify and to answer questions about what has happened in an age appropriate and truthful manner. Again, an awareness of the immediate impact of the homicide on the child's/teen's daily functioning can be more helpful than thinking that questions or support involve a need to know "what happened". By addressing these needs first in our support efforts we may experience a natural and healing unfolding of what else needs to happen to provide support for the family/young person.

Should my child attend the funeral and or participate in the funeral?
Joseph Primo, MDiv, Chief Executive Officer, Good Grief
While it is natural to want to "protect" children from the painful reality of death, end of life rituals are vital to a child's understanding of death and a key component of grief and mourning. Funerals are communal events, which we have been performing since the beginning of time, across continents and cultures. Allowing children the option to attend and participate in these significant end of life rituals is important. Start by telling them what it will look like. Walk them through what they will see, who might come, what people might say, and how people might feel. Children are wonderfully inquisitive and they will be curious at the funeral. Answer questions honestly and confess when you don't know the answer.
Many parents find it helpful to have a point person during the funeral. Identify someone you and your child trust to be available if your child wants to take a break or stop participating in the ritual. So, give kids the facts they need, normalize the experience, and let them know their choices. If they decide they do not want to participate that's okay, too. Just be sure they are making the decision with unbiased facts.

What reactions might I expect to see with my grieving child?
Lauren Schneider, LCSW, Clinical Director of Child and Adolescent Programs, OUR HOUSE Grief Support Center
Your child will grieve in his or her own unique way. How they grieve will depend on many different factors including their age, their stage of cognitive development; cultural influences; their relationship with the deceased and most importantly, how you are grieving. Young children up to age 6 are subject to the kind of illogical or magical thinking typical of that developmental stage. They are also egocentric and may think that somehow they caused the death of their loved one. In addition young children don't understand that death is irreversible and may be waiting for their loved one to return. Young children need reassurance, comfort and patience on your part as you respond their questions. School Aged children understand that death is permanent but still struggle to make sense of what happened. Respond to their questions in truthful, direct language and know that they are old enough to hear the answer if they've asked the question. Children of this age may lack the ability to verbalize their feelings and may behave in ways that cause additional problems. Children may have trouble tolerating strong emotions that are triggered by reminders of the deceased and will need to learn ways to cope with those feelings and thoughts. Parents and caregivers can provide reassurance and bereavement support programs can provide opportunities for children to connect with others who are also coping with a death in the family. Adolescents are also egocentric and struggle with guilt and regret when a loved one dies. They may attempt to cope with their grief in ways that can be impulsive or even unhealthy. In addition to keeping the lines of communication open with their teens, parents and caregivers can promote supportive relationships. Participation in grief support programs with similarly bereaved teens is also beneficial. Families can encourage teens to continue to pursue the goals they'd had before the death, including leaving home for college or work after high school graduation.

How can I help my child transition back to school? When should they go back to school?
Staff at Judi's House and JAG Institute for Grieving Children and Families
Going back to school after a death in the family can be an emotional experience for children, as well as parents and caregivers. Although there isn't a "right" time to go back to school, it is important to promote a return to routine activities and structure. Caregivers should consider the child's level of comfort in being separated from supportive adults, and may want to have children attend half days or come to school for lunch breaks to help ease the transition. It is important to let school personnel know about the death and share what has been helpful to the child. The impact of a family death on a child's academic functioning can be unpredictable. Grief reactions can intensify at any time—including during a math test. In some situations, grief can influence a child's ability to make decisions, and impair memory and concentration, resulting in a decline in school performance. There can also be symptoms similar to ADHD, including disorganization, distractibility, hyperactivity and impulsivity. Grieving students are likely to benefit from additional social, emotional and learning supports. Parents and caregivers may want to request that school personnel consider making additional accommodations for their children, such as opportunities for breaks or time with a counselor during the day, reduced workload or assignment extensions, assistance with organization and time management, or tutoring when needed. Families can advocate for their children by sharing the resources they have found helpful with school personnel.

What are some of the challenges my child may face at school?
Andy McNiel, M.A., Chief Executive Officer, National Alliance for Grieving Children
There are many common challenges kids who are grieving express having at school. Many children might be nervous to return to school because they are worried that others might ask them about their person's death. Some report being distracted and even frustrated because they cannot concentrate on their work. Other children have reported that they are worried they might have a grief trigger and get upset or cry in front of their friends. Some children have also reported being bullied, or picked on by other children; and some simply share that people say things that they intend to be helpful or comforting, but that are actually hurtful. Even with all of these potential challenges, though, school remains a safe, structured environment for children and can be helpful as they adapt to life without their person who died. It is helpful to be with friends, get out of the house, and take part in coordinated, fun activities. Although returning to school can be challenging, parents/caregivers can be encouraging, schedule time to "check-in" about how school is going, and listen when their children need to express their frustrations.

How do I parent a grieving child?
Peter Willig, LMFT, FT, Chief of Operations and Clinical Director Children's Bereavement Center
The experience of grief can be difficult for any child to comprehend and sharing their feelings can be a challenge. After a death, children are often left feeling frightened, angry, sad or confused. They may lack the ability to express themselves, or reach out for help, in a clear or mature way. Often when a child misbehaves they are trying to communicate a need for help, or a strong feeling, and just lack the vocabulary and skills needed. Adults may see negative or "acting out" behavior as intentional, but sometimes it is just a reflection of the child's limitations and desire for support. While no loss experience should excuse antisocial or dangerous behavior, we must not miss the messages in our child's actions. Set clear limits for the negative behavior and focus on safety being absolute, while also offering healthier ways for the child to express himself or herself. Be confident, but not overly critical, when commenting on misbehavior. When a child doesn't want to "talk," parents and caregivers can still model healthy self-expression by sharing their own feelings. When we help children find better ways to share their feelings and needs, negative behaviors are less likely to occur.

Can my child be okay?
Julie Kaplow, Ph.D., Director, Trauma and Grief Center for Youth University of Texas Health Science Center Department of Psychiatry and Behavioral Sciences
After the death of a loved one, parents and caregivers are often concerned about their children's ability to cope. Although the field of childhood grief is still learning about how children function after a death, current research indicates that bereaved youth usually go on to lead healthy and productive lives.

(Continued)

It is also natural to see changes in children's behaviors after a death, including signs of sadness, anger, and fear. That being said, it is helpful to be aware of signs that can tell us when a child may be in need of more formalized, professional support. Some behaviors that might indicate the need for further support include: (1) inability to keep up with daily tasks, such as regularly attending school, completing homework, personal hygiene; (2) significant, ongoing signs of extreme sadness, sobbing, or social withdrawal; (3) risky, harmful behaviors (drug use, reckless driving, stealing); (4) inability to acknowledge the death, or appearing numb or totally disconnected from the reality of the death; or (5) persistent fantasies about ending his/her life in order to be reunited with the deceased person in an afterlife. It is also important for parents and caregivers to trust their instincts about whether their child is struggling excessively to cope in the aftermath of a death. After all, parents are often the true "experts" when it comes to observing uncharacteristic behavioral changes in their own child.

Where can I find support?
Donna A. Gaffney, DNSc, PMHCNS-BC, FAAN, Advisor for Research and Content Development, National Alliance for Grieving Children
Grieving is a natural human experience and serves a crucial purpose in our lives after we lose someone important to us. While the parent-child relationship and open communication are the most important tools to insure healthy adjustment after a family death, many parents have concerns about their children or feel the need for more support for their children or themselves. Fortunately, there are resources for children and families that can promote a child's health after loss. Many communities have support programs for individuals who are grieving. Professionals and trained volunteers provide activities and opportunities for children to be with peers who are also coping with a death. Many programs also provide parent education or group sessions that offer information, support and suggestions for parenting their bereaved children. There are also child and family mental health centers based in health care facilities or universities where experts provide screening and counseling services for children who may be having a more difficult time after the loss. Families can identify resources by asking trusted health care providers for suggestions in their own communities. Public libraries not only contain helpful books for children and parents but may also have listings of regional resources. The National Alliance for Grieving Children is the most comprehensive source for information and services focusing on childhood bereavement. The NAGC website and its Childhood Bereavement Awareness Initiative website contain many resources for families including a listing of grief programs and centers across the United States. Parents and children face new and unfamiliar challenges as they grieve a death in the family; it is a time to gather as many resources as possible.

About the National Alliance for Grieving Children:

The National Alliance for Grieving Children is a 501(c)3 charitable organization that promotes awareness of the needs of children and teens grieving a death and provides education and resources for anyone who wants to support them, because all grieving children deserve a chance to heal. Through the collective voice of our members and partners **we advocate**, **we educate** and **we raise awareness**.

For more information, to find support in your area, or to donate, please visit: **www.ChildrenGrieve.org**

Credits:

Adapted & Authored by:

Stephanie Gunner, MA, LPC joined the NAGC in 2012 and serves as the Program and Communications Coordinator. Formerly a grief counselor, she was the Groups and Resources Coordinator at the Amelia Center in Birmingham, AL where she provided individual and family counseling to bereaved children, parents and families. She holds a Bachelor of Arts in Anthropology from the University of Notre Dame and a Master of Arts in Counseling from the University of Alabama at Birmingham. She resides in Birmingham, Alabama with her husband and four children.

Megan Lopez, LMSW joined the NAGC in 2013 and serves as the National Program Director. Megan has served as a Social Worker and Program Leader throughout her nonprofit career, and has provided support to children, teenagers and families in a variety of settings. She holds a Bachelor of Arts in Social Work from Texas Tech University and Master of Science in Social Work from the University of Texas at Arlington. Megan resides in San Antonio, Texas with her husband and two children.

Andy McNiel, MA joined the NAGC in 2011 and serves as the Chief Executive Officer. Andy has served as a non-profit manager and leader throughout his career, and has provided support and counseling to children, teenagers and adults in a variety of support settings. He holds a Bachelor of Arts in Religion from Palm Beach Atlantic University and Master of Arts in Counseling from the University of Alabama at Birmingham. He is a national trainer for the Boys and Girls Clubs of America and for the American Foundation for Suicide Prevention. He resides in Stuart, Florida with his wife and three children.

Edited by: Donna A. Gaffney, DNSc, PMHCNS-BC, FAAN, A'Lisha Williams, Kathy Wisnefski, Robin Fiorelli, LCSW

Graphic Designer: Stephanie Gunner

Acknowledgments

The staff of the National Alliance for Grieving Children would like to thank the following organizations and individuals who contributed ideas and/or activities for this book:

Greg Adams, LCSW, ACSW, FT of the Center for Good Mourning, Arkansas Children's Hospital | Alesia Alexander Layne, MSW, LCSW, CT | Bo's Place | The Center for Grieving Children in Portland, Maine | The Dougy Center for Grieving Children | Fernside Center for Grieving Children and Families An affiliate of Hospice of Cincinnati | Pamela Gabbay, M.A., FT | Donna A. Gaffney, DNSc, PMHCNS-BC, FAAN | Tony Grace | Amy Hicks of Helping Paws Healing Hearts, Healing Hearts Grief Weekends | Judi's House and JAG Institute for Grieving Children and Families | Julie Kaplow, Ph.D. | Melissa Lunardini M.A., MFT-I | Andrew Paul Maksymowicz | Marian Mankin, LCSW | Susie Munsey of Tu Nidito Children and Family Services | Our House Grief Support Center | Joseph Primo, Mdiv. | Rays of Hope Grief Centre | Rebecca Hobbs-Lawrence | Roberta's House Family Grief Support Center | Lauren Schneider, LCSW | South Nassau Communities Hospital- SIBS®Place: Suzanne Kornblatt, LMSW, Joanna Formont, LMHC and Kerri Wagner, MA, CAT | Kate Thome | A'Lisha Williams | Peter Willig, LMFT, FT,

Lastly, thank you to all of the bereaved children, teens and families who in one capacity or another have intersected our lives and have inspired the creation of this book in the hopes that no child will ever have to feel alone in their grief.

Contributions

Typeface: The text face is Jellygest, designed by Jakob Fischer
Cover: Image compilation of "A single tree stands under rain cloud." © antart/Shutterstock and "Spring blossoming tree. Dreaming girl on swing." © antart/Shutterstock

A Message of Hope to Parents/Caregivers Raising Bereaved Children: Image © Shutterstock: Lucky Team Studio
A Message of Hope to Kids: Butterfly © suns07butterfly/Shutterstock
My Someone Who Died: Concept: Amy Hicks of Helping Paws Healing Hearts & Healing Hearts Grief Weekends; Image © Prapann/Shutterstock
Memories Last Forever: Concept: Our House Grief Support Center, Los Angeles; Image © John T Takai/Shutterstock
A Lasting Impression
Alike and Different: Activity: Kate Thome
Remembering Your Person
(Draw Anything): Concept: Peggy Pettit; Image © Lorelyn Medina/Shutterstock

Understanding Death and Remembering with Ritual Image derivative of "A single tree stands under rain cloud." © antart/Shutterstock
Death is a Part of Life Image © DeepGreen/Shutterstock
What Do You Think?
When People Die Images © John T Takai/Shutterstock
What's That? Images: Mausoleum © germanjames/Shutterstock; Hearse © crwpitman/Shutterstock; Headstone © Martin Haas/Shutterstock; Urn © Boris 15/Shutterstock; Casket © Marko Bradic/Shutterstock; Cemetery © Ad Oculos/Shutterstock; Columbarium © Kenneth E. Varner, CCFE
The Funeral/Memorial Service

What is Grief Like? Image derivative of "A single tree stands under rain cloud." © antart/Shutterstock
Grief is Like... Image © Lorelyn Medina/Shutterstock
My Grief is Like… Concept: Tina Barrett, EdD, LCPC & Molly Pickett, MA of Tamarack Grief Resource Center
My Grief: Agree or Disagree Pencil @ Julia Ivantsova/Shutterstock
Feelings are Physical Bear © Sujono sujono/Shutterstock
Feelings Factory Image © Phil Holmes/Shutterstock
Grief is Full of Surprises Concept of grief triggers: Helen Fitzgerald; Bo's Place; Image© Matthew Cole/Shutterstock
Rainy Days Happen: Concept: Roberta's House Family Grief Support Center; Image © Lorelyn Medina/Shutterstock
The Twists & Turns of Grief Image © VOOK/Shutterstock

My Support...How I Cope with Grief Image derivative of "A single tree stands under rain cloud." © antart/Shutterstock
My Family Concept: South Nassau Communities Hospital- SIBS®Place: Suzanne Kornblatt, LMSW, Joanna Formont, LMHC and Kerri Wagner, MA, CAT
I Am Supported Concept: South Nassau Communities Hospital- SIBS®Place: Suzanne Kornblatt, LMSW, Joanna Formont, LMHC and Kerri Wagner, MA, CAT; A'Lisha Williams,
I Am Brave Image © Igor Zakowski/Shutterstock
All Kinds of Changes Concept: Bo's Place & Susie Munsey of TuNidito Children and Family Services
I Never, I Wonder, I Wish Activity: Pamela Gabbay, M.A., FT & Melissa Lunardini M.A., MFT-I
It's Okay to Feel Sad Concept: OUR HOUSE Grief Support Center; Images: Children © Matthew Cole/Shutterstock; Tissues © Sergiy Kuzmin/Shutterstock; Phone © Chaythawin/Shutterstock; Pillows/Blanket © Sergiy Zavgorodny/Shutterstock; Soup © Nata-Lia/Shutterstock; Album © Vasilyev Alexandr/Shutterstock; Art Supplies © Pozryakov/Shutterstock
It's Ok to Feel Mad Concept: OUR HOUSE Grief Support Center & Rays of Hope Children's Grief Centre; Boy © Matthew Cole/Shutterstock; Phone book © Mega Pixel/Shutterstock; Pillows © Africa Studio/Shutterstock; Scribble © JeremyWhat/Shutterstock; Snowballs © Alexxwy V Smirnov/Shutterstock; Water balloons © Alexy Stiop/Shutterstock; Sports Equipment © Mike Flippo/Shutterstock
Fear Child in Bed © Matthew Cole/Shutterstock; Purple Monster © Albert Ziganshin/Shutterstock; Font on sign: Bangers by Vernon Adams; Cute Monsters © Art'nLera/Shutterstock
Bringing Fears to Light Image © NLshop/Shutterstock
Calming Exercise Flowers © Klara Viskova/Shutterstock; Birthday Cake with Candles © HitToon.Com/Shutterstock
I Like & Dislike Activity: Rebecca Hobbs-Lawrence, The Dougy Center

Grief At School and With Friends Image derivative of "A single tree stands under rain cloud." © antart/Shutterstock
Grief At School Image © Matthew Cole/Shutterstock; Blackboard Font: CHAWP by Tyler Finck
What School is Like for Me Image © Lorelyn Medina/Shutterstock
Hurtful Words Activity: A'Lisha Williams, Image© Matthew Cole/Shutterstock; Call out Font: Bangers by Vernon Adams
Responding to Hurtful Words Image© Matthew Cole/Shutterstock; Font in boxes: Myriad Pro
Helpful Words Activity: A'Lisha Williams, Image© Matthew Cole/Shutterstock; Call out Font: Myriad Pro
What Comforts You? Activity: Fernside Center for Grieving Children and Families, An affiliate of Hospice of Cincinnati; Sun © Thodoris Tibilis/Shutterstock; Children © Lorelyn Medina/Shutterstock; Banner font: Dadhand by Tepid Monkey Fonts
(Draw Anything): Concept: Peggy Pettit; Image © Lorelyn Medina/Shutterstock

Special Days and Remembering My Person Image derivative of "A single tree stands under rain cloud." © antart/Shutterstock
Special Days & Holidays Image © makeitdouble/Shutterstock
Remembering...My Way
Remembering...As a Family
A Letter to Your Person Concept: Bo's Place & Greg Adams, LCSW, ACSW, FT, Center for Good Mourning, Arkansas Children's Hospital; Children © Lorelyn Medina/Shutterstock; Paper © Nuttapong/Shutterstock
A Letter from Your Person to You Concept: Bo's Place & Greg Adams, LCSW, ACSW, FT, Center for Good Mourning, Arkansas Children's Hospital; Children © Lorelyn Medina/Shutterstock; Paper © Nuttapong/Shutterstock; Font on letter: Dadhand by Tepid Monkey Fonts
Map of Grief Concept: Tony Grace; Treasure Map & Pop Up Book with a Pirate Theme © Lorelyn Medina/Shutterstock; Landforms © aekikuis/Shutterstock; Treasure Chest, Ship, Sharks, Island, Waves, Whirlpool, Octopus © Lorelyn Medina/Shutterstock; Background paper © Cranach/Shutterstock; Waterfall & House © Matthew Cole/Shutterstock; Volcano © Sign N Symbol Production/Shutterstock; Compass © Polovinkin/Shutterstock
(Draw Anything): Concept: Peggy Pettit; Image © Lorelyn Medina/Shutterstock
A Year in Review Concept: The Center for Grieving Children, Portland Maine
Game Time! Concept: Andrew Paul Maksymowicz; Imagen derivado de "A boardgame with kids and buildings" and "Illustration of houses, and other buildings" © GraphicsRF/Shutterstock
Closing Message to Kids Notebook, Pencils © Matthew Cole/Shutterstock; Heart © National Alliance for Grieving Children

© National Alliance for Grieving Children 2016